M000024622

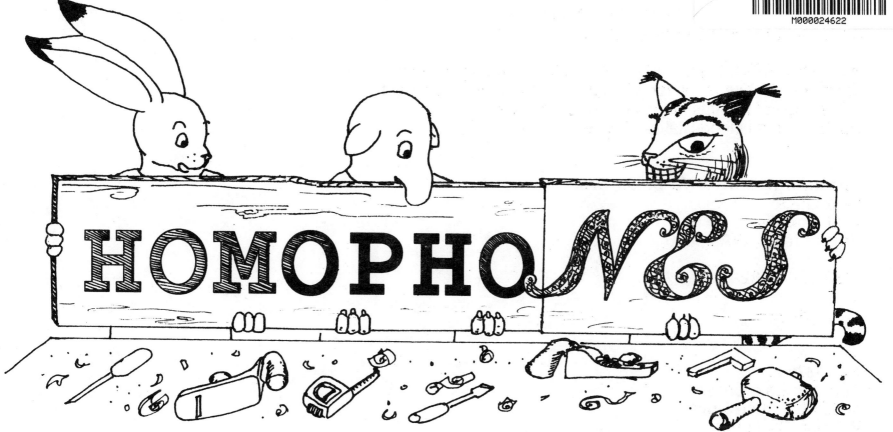

An Illustrated Dictionary

803 Common and Unusual Pairs, Trios, and Quads,
of Words with Different Meanings and Spellings
That Sound Alike

compiled by Irene Soohoo
illustrated by Annarie Buxman

Homophones: An Illustrated Dictionary
© Copyright 1995 by Irene Soohoo

All rights reserved. No part of this book may be reproduced
in any manner whatsoever without written permission except
in the case of reprints in the context of reviews.
Printed in the United States of America

For information or to place orders, write to
Lynx Links
P. O. Box 754
Brush Prairie, WA 98606

(360)256-8332

Publisher:
Peacock Enterprises
10333 Lundene Drive
Whittier, CA 90601

ISBN 0-937673-10-2

**Dedicated to my eighth grade Language Arts class
in Amboy, Washington,**

especially

Justin Allen
Ethan Kysar
Julia Olson
Jason Tikka
Erin Wheatley

Thanks to

Tim Benton
Wilberta Chinn
Gina Garlie
Kelly Hall
Ric Soohoo

for help and
encouragement

Homophones sound the same but have **different spellings and meanings**.

Spellings variations are different ways of spelling the same words with the same meanings.
Homographs have the same spellings with different meanings.
Homonyms can be homophones or homographs. This is a collection of **homophones**.

Entries are in alphabetical order by the first homophone in the group.

Introducing:

Kenia the Lynx   Oscar the Tapir   Sid the Hare

docile\DOS ul\ adj. teachable, tame
dossal\DOS ul\ n. an ornamental cloth
on the back of a throne, also **dossel, dorsal**

Abbreviations

adj.   adjective
adv.   adverb
conj.   conjunction
interj.   interjection
n.   noun
prep.   preposition
pron.   pronoun
v.   verb

Stressed Syllable Capitalized

baby \BAY bee\
call \KAHL\

Simplified Guide to Pronunciation

\a\   as in cat
\ah\   as in father, hot
\air\   as in fair, care, wear
\ar\   as in far
\ay\   as in day, main

\e\   as in egg
\ee\   as in meet, beat, ski, happy
\er\   as in fern, were, bird, worst, murder

\i\   as in igloo
\I\   as in ice, fly

\o\   as in hot
\oh\   as in oh, doe, joke
\oy\   as in boy, oil
\or\   as in for, bore
\ou\   as in out, cow

\u\   as in up
\oo\   as in moon
\uh\   as in until

\y\   as in yellow
\th\   as in bath
\TH\   as in bathe
\ch\   as in chip
\sh\   as in shop
\st\   as in still

lynx   links

1   **acanthous**\uh KAN thus\ adj. having spines
acanthus\uh KAN thus\ n. a prickly herb
of the Mediterranean area

2   **ad**\AD\ n. advertisement
add\AD\ n. to join, to combine

3   **aerie**\AIR ee\ n. a nest or dwelling
on a cliff, also eyrie\I ree\ or \EE ree\
aery\AIR ee\ adj. ethereal, intangible
airy\AIR ee\ adj. breezy

acanthous

4   **affront**\uh FRUNT\ n. an insult
v. to insult, to offend
afront\uh FRUNT\ adv. abreast

airy

ai

aye

6   **aid**\AYD\ n. help   v. to help
      aide\AYD\ n. an assistant

7   **aiel**\AYL\ n. a writ for an
      estate brought by an heir
      ail\AYL\ v. to suffer ill health
      ale\AYL\ n. a fermented drink
      made with malt and hops

ale

ail

5   **ai**\I\ n. a three-toed sloth
      ay\I\ interj. an expression of sorrow
      aye\I\ adv. yes
      eye\I\ n..an organ of sight
      I\I\ pron. the one who is speaking,
      9th letter of the alphabet

eye

air

8 **ain**\AYN\ n. Scottish meaning one,
adj. a British word for own
ayn\AYN\ n. 18th letter of the
Arabic alphabet, also **ayin**\I un\

9 **air**\AYR\ n. the invisible
gases we breathe
e'er\AYR\ adv. ever, also \ER\
ere\AYR\ adv. early, soon   conj. before
err\E(e)r\ v. to make a mistake,
eyre\A uh er\ n. a medieval,
English circuit court
heir\E(e)r\ n. one who inherits

err

heir

10 **airing**\AIR ing\ n. ventilation,
exposure to air, public discussion,
a regular radio or television broadcast
erring\AIR ing\ adj. misbehaving

11 **aisle\I ul** n. a passageway
between sections of seats or rows
I'll\I ul contraction for I will, I shall
isle\I ul n. island

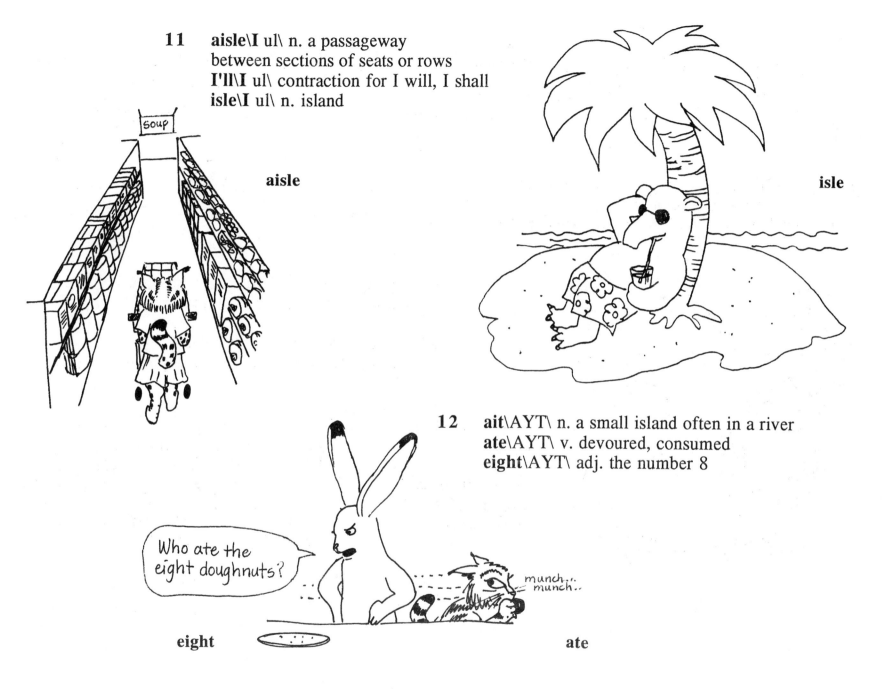

aisle

isle

12 **ait\AYT** n. a small island often in a river
ate\AYT v. devoured, consumed
eight\AYT adj. the number 8

Who ate the
eight doughnuts?

munch...
munch..

eight

ate

awl

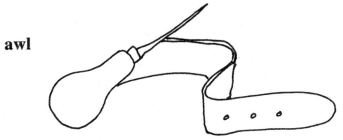

13 **all**\AHL\ adj. every part   adv. altogether
pron. the whole amount
awl\AHL\ n. a tool for making small holes

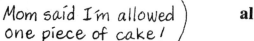

allowed

14 **allay**\uh LAY\ v. to reduce, to relieve
allee\uh LAY\ n. a walkway or mall

15 **allo**\A loh\ adj. closely related
aloe\AL oh\ n. tonic from a lily family plant

allot

16 **allot**\uh LOT\ v.
to assign
a share not
necessarily equal
a lot\uh LOT\ adj.
much, many

a lot

aloud

17 allowed\uh LOUD\ v. permitted
aloud\uh LOUD\ adv. out loud

18 altar\AL ter\ n. place for sacrifice or worship
alter\AL ter\ v. to change, to spay

19 anil\AN il\ n. a West Indian shrub
from which indigo dye is made
anile\AN il\ adj. like a feeble,
old woman

altar

alter

20 ant\ANT\ n. an insect
aunt\ANT\ n. sister of your mother
or father, wife of your uncle

This is my sister, your Aunt Carol.

Hello, Oscar.

ant

aunt

21 **apatite**\AP uh tit\ n. group of calcium phosphate minerals often occurring as hexagonal crystals
appetite\AP uh tit\ n. the desire to eat

22 **Appalachian**\ap puh LAY chun\ adj. of or pertaining to a mountain range in the eastern U.S.
appellation\ap puh LAY shun\ n. the act of making an appeal, the act of calling a name

23 **appressed**\uh PREST\ adj. pressed flat
oppressed\uh PREST\ v. crushed by tyranny

24 **arc**\ARK\ n. something curved
ark\ARK\ n. a boat

25 **aura**\OR uh\ n. a halo, atmosphere
ora\OR uh\ n. Danish money introduced into England in 920 A.D., mouths, plural of **os**

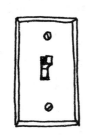

on

26 **auto**\AH toh\ n. automobile
otto\AH toh\ n. a perfume, also **attar**\AT er\

27. **awn**\ON\ n. slender bristles on cereal grasses
on\ON\ adj. planned, operating, taking place
adv. verb plus on   prep. in contact with

28 **axel**\AK sul\ n. an ice skating jump
axil\AK sul\ n. an angle between the
stem and leaf or trunk and branch
axle\AK sul\ n. a shaft between a pair of wheels

29 **b**\BEE\ n. the letter, the grade
be\BEE\ v. shows state of being
bee\BEE\ n. a honey-making insect,
a spelling contest, quiltmaking session,
a piece of wood to tie down a sail

bee

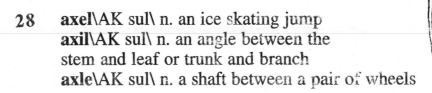

awn

baa

bah

bail

30   **baa**\BAH\ n. the bleat of a sheep, also **ba**
        bah\BAH\ interj. used to express disgust

31   **baal**\BAYL\ n. local Canaanite or Phoenician gods
        bail\BAYL\ n. money given for the release of a
        prisoner, an animal pen, a half hoop on a pail,
        a hinged bar that holds paper
        against the platen of a typewriter,
        to throw water out of a boat,
        to parachute
        out of an airplane
        bale\BAYL\ n.
        a large bundle
        pressed and tied   **bail**
        v. to make
        into a bale

32 babble\BAB ul\ n. foolish talk
v. to make meaningless sounds
babel\BAB ul\ n. a confusion of speech

33 bach\BACH\ v. to live like a bachelor
batch\BACH\ n. the amount baked
or made at one time

bad

I could feel bad about my bad back and the bad things in life, but I'd rather count my blessings...

34 bad\BAD\ adj. poor, evil,
n. an unhappy state
bade\BAD\ v. said

35 bade\BAYD\ v. said
bayed\BAYD\ v. howled

36 baetyl\BEED ul\ n. a meteorite worshipped as a sacred stone
beetle\BEED ul\ n. an insect, a heavy hammer, a machine
that gives a lustrous finish to fabric   v. to loom over

37 baht\BOT\ n. current Thai money
bot\BOT\ n. a sponger, the parasitic larva of the botfly
that lays eggs on horses, also **bott**   v. to borrow and not repay
bought\BOT\ v. purchased, paid for
adj. ready made "store bought"

38 bailee\BAY lee\ n. the person given goods for security
bailey\BAY lee\ n. the outer wall of a castle or the space
between two outer walls
bailie\BAY lee\ n. a Scot. magistrate, bailiff, also **baillie**

39 bain\BAYN\ adj. supple, ready, near
bane\BAYN\ n. a curse, death   v. to harm

40   **bairn**\BA urn\ n. a Scottish child
baron\BAIR un\ n. a nobleman
barren\BAIR un\ adj. bare, fruitless

41   **bait**\BAYT\ n. something to put on a hook
or in a trap   v. to lure, to provoke
bate\BAYT\ v. to reduce the force

42   **baize**\BAYZ\ n. wool or cotton imitating felt
bays\BAYZ\ n. inlets of the sea, compartments
in a building or ship   v. howls

bait

bawled

43   **bald**\BAHLD\ adj. without hair, white markings
balled\BAHLD\ adj. rolled or wadded into a ball
bawled\BAHLD\ v. cried, wailed, scolded

44   **baldie**\BAHLD ee\ n. a double-ended
Scottish fishing boat
baldy\BAHLD ee\ n. a white-headed
Australian pigeon

45   **balk**\BAHK\ n. an unplowed ridge of land
between fields   v. to refuse to go on,
to stop in middle of pitching a ball,
to block, also **baulk**
bock\BAHK\ n. a dark, rich beer

ball

46 **ball**\BAHL\ n. a sphere, a toy,
a formal dance, a good time
bawl\BAHL\ v. to cry n. a loud cry

47 **balm**\BAHM\ n. a soothing ointment,
resin from a tropical evergreen
bomb\BAHM\ n. an explosive device,
a rounded mass of lava, a lead container
for radioactive material   v. to attack with bombs

barred

I'm innocent!
I was framed!
Let me out!

bard

48 **bard**\BARD\ n. a singing poet, a piece of armor
for a horse's neck, also **barde**
barred\BARD\ adj. marked with stripes, blocked

49 **bare**\BAIR\ adj. without covering   v. to uncover
bear\BAIR\n. a large, heavy coated mammal, a seller
of stock who expects the price to go down
v. to carry, to give birth, to tolerate pain

bear

50 **bark**\BARK\ n. the sound of a
dog's cry, the outer covering of trees
barque\BARK\ n. a three masted
sailing ship, also **barkentine** or
barquentine

51. **base**\BAYS\ n. the bottom of something, a starting place, a salt adj. vile, indecent
bass\BAYS\ n. a deep, low sound, a person with a low voice, a stringed musical instrument adj. low toned

bass

baste

base

I rented the movie "The Color Purple." It's based on a book by Alice Walker.

"The Color Purple" was a book?

52. **based**\BAYST\ v. founded on, started on, situated
baste\BAYST\ v. to sew with long, loose stitches v. to moisten meat with drippings while cooking, to scold

based

53   **bask**\BASK\ v. to lie in the sun or in a warm place, to enjoy
basque\BASK\ n. a shirtlike continuation of a doublet,
a bodice on a Basque woman's costume

54   **bay**\BAY\ adj. reddish brown color   n. an inlet of the sea v. to howl
bey\BAY\ n. a Turkish governor

bizarre

bazaar

55   **bazaar**\buh ZAR\ n. rows of shops or stalls
for selling goods, a charity function
bizarre\buh ZAR\ adj. weird, sensational, atypical

beach

56   beach\BEECH\ n. the shore
by a body of water   v. to run aground
beech\BEECH\ n. a hardwood tree with edible nuts

beech

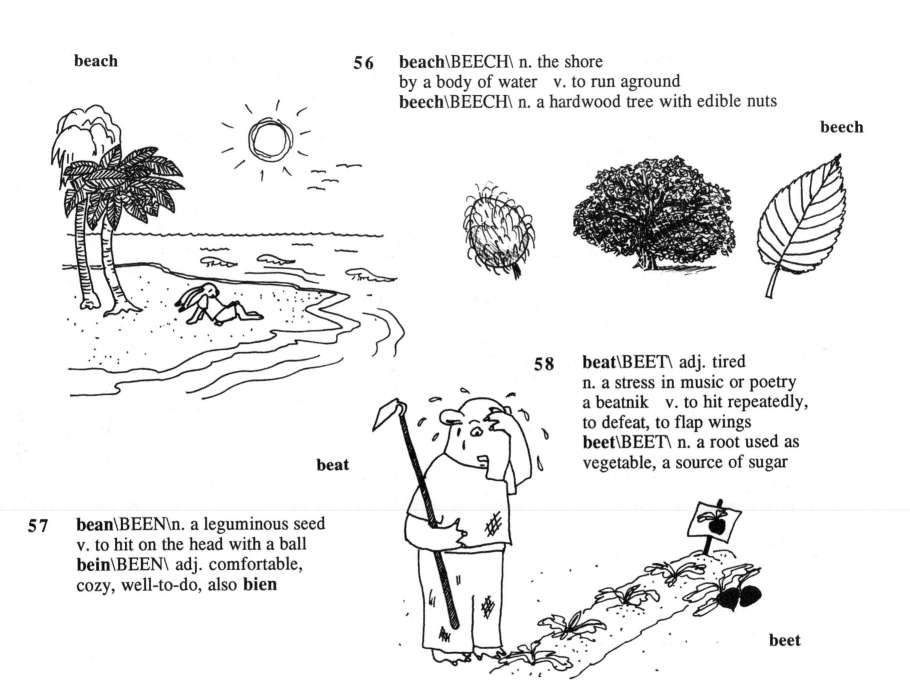

beat

58   beat\BEET\ adj. tired
n. a stress in music or poetry
a beatnik   v. to hit repeatedly,
to defeat, to flap wings
beet\BEET\ n. a root used as
vegetable, a source of sugar

57   bean\BEEN\n. a leguminous seed
v. to hit on the head with a ball
bein\BEEN\ adj. comfortable,
cozy, well-to-do, also **bien**

beet

beau   **bow**   59

beer

beau\BOH\ n. boyfriend, steady escort
bow\BOH\ n. weapon used to shoot arrows,
a knot doubling in loops, a rod for playing
the violin, something bent into a curve

60   beaux\BOHZ\ n. boyfriends
bows\BOHZ\ n. looped knots,
weapons to shoot arrows, rods

61   been\BIN\ v. past form of to be
bin\BIN\ n. a box or container

bin

62   beer\BEER\ n. a malted,
alcoholic beverage
bier\BEER\ n. a stand for a coffin
or the stand and coffin together

63 **bees**\BEEZ\ n. honey-making insects
bise\BEEZ\ n. a cold, dry north wind
of southern France, Italy, and Switzerland

64 **bel**\BEL\ n. ten decibels, a thorny tree of India
bell\BEL\ n. a hollow metal device that rings,
a bellow or roar v. to provide with a bell, to bay
belle\BEL\ n. a beautiful girl or woman

belle

bell

65   **berley**\BER lee\ n. ground bait
burley\BER lee\ n. a thin-bodied air cured Kentucky tobacco
burly\BER lee\ adj. husky, strongly and heavily built

bury

66   **berried**\BER eed\ adj. bearing eggs, having berries, also \BAIR eed\
buried\BER eed\ v. covered with earth, also \BAIR eed\

67   **berry**\BER ee\ n. fruit from various vines, a fish or lobster egg, also \BAIR ee\
bury\BER ee\ v. to cover with dirt in a hole, to hide, also \BAIR ee\

berry

berth

68 **berth**\BERTH\ n. a place to sleep on a ship or train, a job, a distance allowed for safety
v. to move into a space
birth\BERTH\ n. coming to life   v. to begin

69 **beurre**\BER\ n. butter
birr\BER\ n. a rush of wind
v. to make a whirring sound
buhr\BER\ n. a buhrstone millstone
burr\BER\ n. a prickly envelope around fruit,
a cutting tool, a rounded irregular mass,
a trilled r in speech

birr

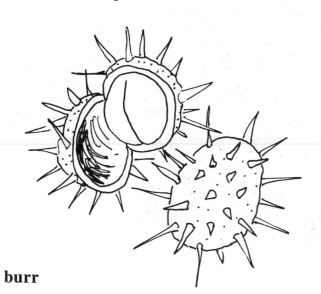

burr

70 **bhut**\BOOT\ n. a devil, a mean spirit
boot\BOOT\ n. footwear that covers the ankle
or leg, money or goods given to complete a deal,
in England, a car's trunk   v. to kick

bight　　**bite**

71　**bight**\BIT\ n. a loop of rope or reins,
a bend in a river, a bay made
by the shoreline
bite\BIT\ n. a mouthful of food, a cut
v. to grip with teeth, to sting,
to cut into, to nip
byte\BIT\ n. computer bits

72　**birdie**\BER dee\ n. a little bird, a golf
score one under par　v. to score
one under par
birdy\BER dee\ adj. full of birds

73　**birl**\BERL\ v. to pour, to spin
burl\BERL\ n. a hemispherical growth on a tree
v. to finish cloth by trimming loose threads

burl

birl

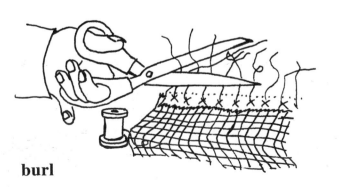

burl

74 **birn**\BERN\ n. a pear-shaped socket
for a woodwind's mouthpiece
burn\BERN\ n. an injury from a burn,
a brook   v. to be on fire, to scorch

75 **bisk**\BISK\ n. an extra turn in croquet, a handicap
for good players and an allowance for inferior players
bisque\BISK\ adj. the c   s brownish pink to
yellowish gray   n. fired but unglazed ceramics, a seafood soup

blend

76 **bit**\BIT\ n. the steel part of a bridle
that goes in a horse's mouth, a drill
bitt\BIT\ n. a post on the deck of a ship
for mooring ropes   v. to tie to a mooring post

bit

77 **bladder**\BLAD er\ n. a sac in animals for urine
blatter\BLAD er\ v. to talk fast and loudly

78 **blastie**\BLAST ee\ n. a disgusting elf or dwarf
blasty\BLAST ee\ adj. subject to gusts of wind

79 **blend**\BLEND\ n. a mix   v. to mix
blende\BLEND\ n. metallic sulfides
with a bright nonmetallic luster

blew

80 **blew**\BLOO\ v. moved with wind or air, gusted
blue\BLOO\ adj. feeling low, indecent
adj. the color or a clear sky

boar

bore

81   **boar**\BOR\ n. a male pig
      bore\BOR\ n. the interior tube of a gun,
      the caliber of a gun, a tidal flood,
      a tiresome person
      v. to drill a hole, to tire out

bore

bore

bored

82 **board**\BORD\ n. sawed lumber
bored\BORD\ v. drilled, tired out

board

83 **bole**\BOHL\ n. tree trunk
boll\BOHL\ n. seed capsule
bowl\BOHL\ n. a deep often round dish, any of several intercollegiate
football games, an outdoor concert theater
v. to play a game with a ball and ten pins

84 **born**\BORN\ adj. brought into existence
borne\BORN\ v. carried, endured, also **born**
bourn\BORN\ n. a stream or brook, a boundary, also **bourne**

burro

85   **borough**\BER oh\ n. houses forming a town, a town corporation
burgh\BER oh\ n. an incorporated Scottish town
burro\BER oh\ n. a donkey
burrow\BER oh\ n. an animal's home made from a hole
in the ground, a den   v. to tunnel, to hide by tunneling

burrow

bough

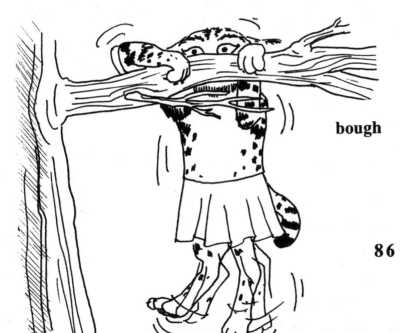

bow

86   **bough**\BOU\ n. a tree limb
bow\BOU\ n. accepting applause,
the forward part of a ship .
v. to bend the head or body forward
to show respect or accept applause

87   **bra**\BRAH\ n. a brassiere
braw\BRAH\ adj. pleasant, splendid

88   **bracken**\BRAK un\ n. coarse ferns, also **braken**
breacan\BRAK un\ n. Scottish Highland plaid,
also **brechan**

breacan

bracken

bray

89   **brae**\BRAY\ n. Scottish hillside along a river
brais\BRAY\ n. medieval breeches
bray\BRAY\ n. the cry of a donkey   v. to make
a donkey's cry, to crush or spread thinly
brey\BRAY\ v. to soften leather
by working with the hands

brake

91   **brake**\BRAYK\ n. a stopping device,
a machine for separating flax
or forming metal, ferns, marshy land
v. to slow or stop
break\BRAYK\ v. to cut, to escape,
to train, to crush the spirit
of an animal, to break a record or a code,
to break into laughter

break

90 braise\BRAYZ\ v. to cook in fat and a little water in a covered pot
brays\BRAYZ\ v. cries, grinds, crushes, spreads
braze\BRAYZ\ v. to solder metal

92 brassie\BRAS ee\ n. wooden golf clubs, also brassey
brassy\BRAS ee\ adj. loud, shrill

braise

breach

breech

93 breach\BREECH\ n. a gap   v. to break into or over,
to leap out of the water
breech\BREECH\ adj. butt first   n. pants, the wooden part of a rifle

bread

94 **bread**\BRED\ n. baked food made from flour
bred\BRED\ v. raised, mated

bred

breed

95 **bream**\BRIM\ n. sunfish, bluegill, also \BREEM\
brim\BRIM\ n. the rim of a container

96 **brede**\BREED\ n. embroidery, braiding and weaving of colors
breed\BREED\ n. a group of related plants or animals
with common characteristics   v. to raise, to mate

97 **bree**\BREE\ n. broth, liquor
Brie\BREE\ n. a soft French cheese

98 **brevet**\BREV ut\ n. official government permission,
an honorary military rank given by the President
for distinguished service, also \bre VET\
brevit\BREV ut\ v. to pry, to snoop

brede

99   brew\BROO\ n. a steeped and fermented beverage   v. to plot, to cook
broo\BROO\ n. a favorable opinion
bruh\BROO\ n. a pigtailed macaque monkey of the East Indies

100   brewis\BROOZ\ n. beef broth, bread soaked in broth, drippings, or milk
brews\BROOZ\ n. fermented beverages v. plots, cooks
bruise\BROOZ\ n. an injury under the skin without breaking it   v. to dent, to injure

broom

101   bricks\BRIKS\ n. clay compressed into rectangular shapes, baked. and used for building walls and walkways
brix\BRIKS\ n. a hydrometer scale for measuring sugar solutions, often capitalized

bricks

102   bridal\BRIDE ul\ adj. having to do with a wedding or bride
bridle\BRIDE ul\ n. the headstall and reins for a horse

I hope I can find my way home in this fog!

103   broom\BROOM\ n. heather, bundle of fibers sewn together for sweeping   v. to sweep with a broom
brume\BROOM\ n.. fog or mist

brume

104   **brownie\BROUN ee** n. a good natured goblin,
a Girl Scout aged 7 to 9, a flat cakelike chocolate dessert
browny\BROUN ee adj. browned

105   **brows\BROUZ** n. eyebrows,
projecting parts of a cliff
browse\BROUZ n. tender shoots
and leaves used for cattle feed, also **browze**
v. to graze, to skim over, to look but not buy

brows

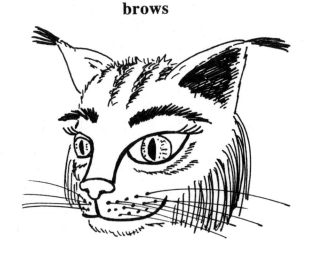

Hmm, this might be a good book...

browse

browse

106   **bruit\BROOT** n. a favorable report, a rumor   v. to report
brut\BROOT adj. dry champagne   n. any of several medieval
English chronicles
brute\BROOT adj. cruel, crude, purely physical   n. a beast

107   **bubalis\BYOO buh lus** n. an African antelope
bubalus\BYOO buh lus n. an Asian mud-wallowing buffalo

108.   **buccal\BUK ul** adj. having to do with cheeks
buckle\BUK ul n. a device to fasten a belt or strap

109 **buckie**\BUK ee\ n. a red whelk seashell
used to make purple dye
bucky\BUK ee\ adj. acting like an uncastrated buck

buss

110 **bus**\BUS\ n. a large passenger vehicle,
an electrical tube
v. to travel by bus, to clear, clean,
and reset tables at a restaurant
buss\BUS\ n. a kiss   v. to kiss

 bus

111 **but**\BUT\ adv. only, merely   conj. except for   prep.without
n. a Scottish kitchen and living quarters of a two room cottage
butt\BUT\ n. a blow or thrust with head or horns, the thicker
end of something, an unused remainder   v. to strike with head
or horns, to join end to end without overlapping

butt

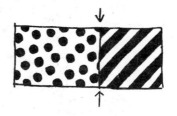

butt

buy

buy\BI\ n.. a purchase   v. to purchase, to pay for
by\BI\ prep. next to, near, via, not later than, past,
following the rules, extent of win, function of multiplication
and measurement (2 by 4)
bye\BI\ adj. off the main route, also **by**   n. in a tournament when
you have no opponent, good-bye

by

113   **buyer**\BI er\ n. one who pays for or purchases
byre\BI er\ n. a cow barn

buyer

byre

114 cache\KASH\ n. a hiding place, storage   v. to hide, to store
cash\KASH\ n. ready money, money paid at the time, a Chinese coin
v. to pay cash, to get cash in exchange for a check or chips

115 caesar\SEEZ er\ n. a dictator
seizor\SEEZ er\ n. one who takes
a freeholder's estate

cache

cash

call

116 call\KAHL\ n. a shout, a ruling on a game
v. to speak, to visit, to request to come,
to rule on a player or game, to demand payment
caul\KAHL\ n. large fatty omentum
covering the intestines, fetal membrane

117 caller\KAHL er\ n. one who calls instructions
or numbers (square dancing or bingo)
collar\KAHL er\ n. a band around the neck

118 came\KAYM\ v. arrived, attended
kame\KAYM\ n. a hill of stratified material deposited by a glacier

119 can\KAN\ n. a cylindrical metal container
v. to be able to do, to permit
khan\KAN\ n. a medieval Chinese ruler,
a ruler of central Asia, an Asian rest house, also \KAHN\

cannon

120 **cannon**\KAN un\ n. a big gun, the bone beneath
the knee in horses and other animals, a carom
in billiards, the ear by which a bell is hung, also **canon**
v. to shoot a cannon, to carom in billiards, to run into
canon\KAN un\ n. a dogma or decree, a clergyman

121 **cant**\KANT\ adj. lively, slanted   n. a corner
of a building, affected speech, phrasing of a
religious sect, a slanting surface   v. to tilt up
can't\KANT\ contraction for can not
quinte\KANT\ n. fifth defensive fencing position

122 **canter**\KANT er\ n. one that talks cant, a beggar
v. to lope, a three beat horse gait
cantor\KANT er\ n. a choir or synagogue leader

123 **caph**\KOF\ n. the 11th letter
of the Hebrew alphabet, also **kaf, kaph**
cough\KOF\ n. an expelling of air
from the lungs   v. to cough

124 **capital**\KAP i tul\ adj. punishable by death, big letter,
most important   n. the value of accumulated goods,
a big letter, the city that is the seat of government,
the top part of a column
capitol\KAP i tul\ n. the building of a state legislature
or the U.S. Congress

capitol

If $10 million is spent on agricultural research...

But taxpayers think...

capital

carat

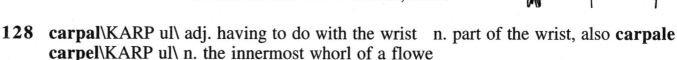

carrot

125 car\KAR\ n. an automobile, an elevator cage, a vehicle
carr\KAR\ adj. Scottish for lefthanded
v. a marsh, an alder grove

126 carat\KAIR ut\ n. a unit of weight
for precious stones, less often **karat**
caret\KAIR ut\ n. an insertion mark
carrot\KAIR ut\ n. a long, orange edible root
karat\KAIR ut\ n. a unit of fineness of gold
equal to 1/24 pure gold, also **carat**

127 caries\KAIR eez\ n. tooth decay
carries\KAIR eez\ v. moves, holds

128 carpal\KARP ul\ adj. having to do with the wrist   n. part of the wrist, also **carpale**
carpel\KARP ul\ n. the innermost whorl of a flowe

129 carry\KAIR ee\ v. to move a load, to transfer
karri\KAIR ee\ n. an Australian eucalyptus tree, also **kari**

130 cart\KART\ n. a wheeled basket for shopping, a two-wheeled vehicle
pulled by a horse or dog   v. to carry in a cart
carte\KART\ n. a card, a bill of fare
quarte\KART\ n. 4th defensive fencing position

131 cask\KASK\ n. a barrel
casque\KASK\ n. head armor, hat shaped like a helmet

132 cast\KAST\ n. something formed in a mold, actors in a play, a tinge, a throw
v. to throw with force, to project, to select an actor for a role in a play
caste\KAST\ n. any of the hereditary Hindu social classes, rigid class distinctions

caught

133 catch\KACH\ \KECH\ n. the total fish caught at one time, a game of tossing a ball back and forth   v. to trap, to discover, to take hold of, to get on board in time
ketch\KECH\ n. a two-masted sailboat

134 caudle\KOD ul\ n. a warm drink for an invalid made with wine mixed with eggs, bread, sugar, and spices
coddle\KOD ul\ v. to pamper, to spoil
katel\KOD ul\ n. an African hammock used as a bed

135 caught\KOT\ v. seized, held, got on board
cot\KOT\ n. a small portable bed made of canvas over a frame, a small house, a cover
xat\KOT\ n. a carved pole memorial put up by some North American Indians

cot

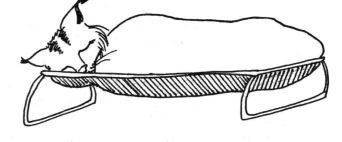

136 caulk\KOK\ n. a piece of metal screwed into horseshoes to prevent slipping on grass
v. to make watertight by filling seams, also **calk**
cock\KOK\ n. an adult male chicken or other fowl, a faucet, a hammer in a lock of a gun, a swaggering person, a tilt, a small pile of hay   v. to draw back a gun's hammer, to tip one's head to one side, to put hay into small piles

cock

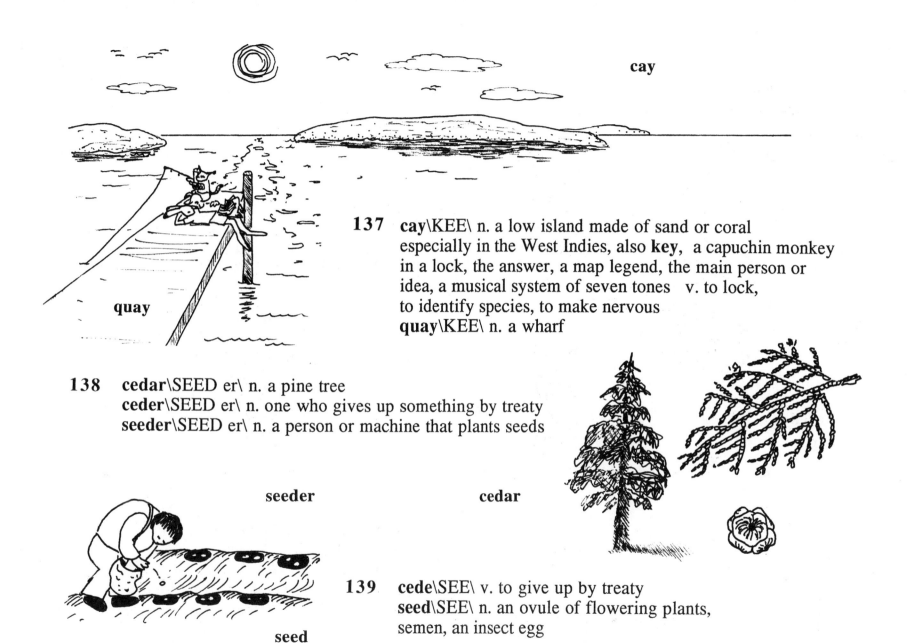

cay

quay

seeder

cedar

seed

137 cay\KEE\ n. a low island made of sand or coral especially in the West Indies, also **key,** a capuchin monkey in a lock, the answer, a map legend, the main person or idea, a musical system of seven tones v. to lock, to identify species, to make nervous
quay\KEE\ n. a wharf

138 cedar\SEED er\ n. a pine tree
ceder\SEED er\ n. one who gives up something by treaty
seeder\SEED er\ n. a person or machine that plants seeds

139 cede\SEE\ v. to give up by treaty
seed\SEE\ n. an ovule of flowering plants, semen, an insect egg

140   ceded\SEED ud\ v. gave up by treaty
seeded\SEED ud\ v. planted seeds

sea

see

ceded

141   cee\SEE\ n. the letter c
sea\SEE\ n. an ocean, a body of salty water
see\SEE\ v. to use your eyes
n. the territory of a bishop

ceil

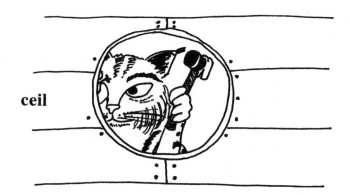

seal

142   ceil\SEEL\ v. to line a ship with planks,
to furnish with a ceiling
seal\SEEL\ n. a marine, carnivorous
mammal, the face of a ring that makes a mark,
a lock v. to hunt seals, to make a mark, to close
seel\SEEL\ v. to sew eyelids shut

ceiling

sealing

143 **ceiling**\SEEL ing\ n. the overhead lining inside a room, the height from the ground to the lowest layer of clouds
sealing\SEEL ing\ v. securing, closing

cell

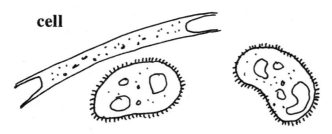

144 **cell**\SEL\ n. a small mass of protoplasm, a small one-room unit
sell\SEL\ v. to exchange for money, to convince   n. a deliberate hoax
selle\SEL\ n. archaic for saddle

cellar

seller

145 **cellar**\SEL er\ n. basement, a stock of wines
sellar\SEL er\ adj. involving the site of the pituitary gland, the selle turica
seller\SEL er\ n. one who sells

sell

146 cense\SENS\ v. to perfume with incense
by swinging a censer
sense\SENS\ n. the ability to see, hear, smell, taste,
or feel; judgement   v. to be aware of, to detect

cense

sense

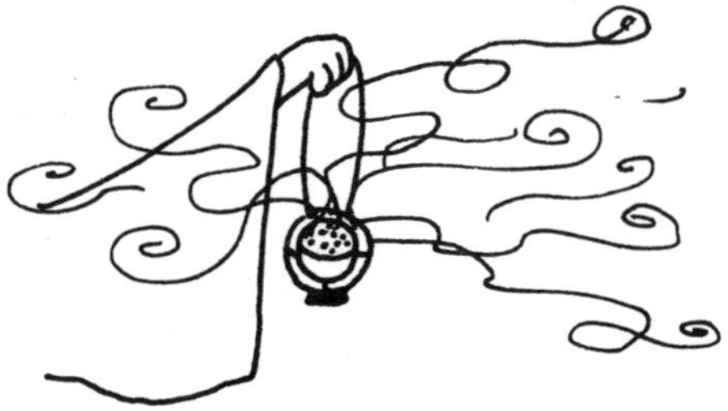

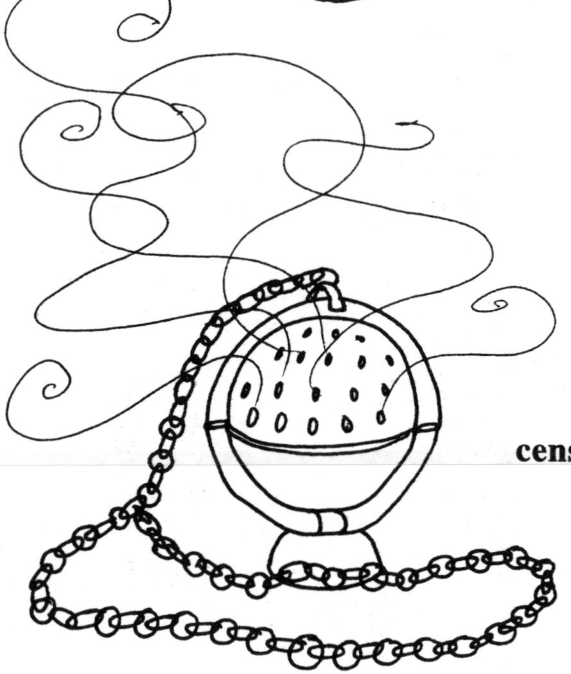

censer

147 censer\SENS er\ n. an incense burner
censor\SENS er\ n. one who removes
forbidden material
sensor\SENS er\ n. a device that detects
or reacts to heat or light

148 censual\SEN shoo ul\ adj. relating to a census, containing a census roll
sensual\SEN shoo ul\ adj. relating to the enjoyment of the senses

cent

scent

sent

149 **cent**\SENT\ n. a penny, 1/100 of a U.S. or Canadian dollar
scent\SENT\ n. an odor, a perfume   v. to smell
sent\SENT\ v. mailed, delivered, thrown, driven

150 **cents**\SENtS\ n. pennies
scents\SENtS\ n. perfumes v. sniffs, smells

151 **cerate**\SAIR ayt\ n. a medicine made from wax mixed with lard
serrate\SAIR ayt\ adj. notched or toothed on the edge

152 **cere**\SEER\ n. a part of a bird's bill,
v. to cover with wax, to wrap in waxed cloth
sear\SEER\ n. a scar left from a burn,
the catch on the hammer of a gun
v. to burn
seer\SEER\ n. a person
who predicts the future

sear

153   **cereal**\SEER ee ul\ n. a food grain
serial\SEER ee ul\ adj. one in a series,
belonging to work appearing regularly

154   **cerous**\SEER us\ adj. having to do
with the metallic element cerium
cirrous\SEER us\ adj. resembling cirrus clouds
cirrus\SEER us\ n. a flexible animal appendage,
a wispy cloud formed at 20,000-40,000 feet
serous\SEER us\ adj. thin and watery like serum

cereal

cirrus

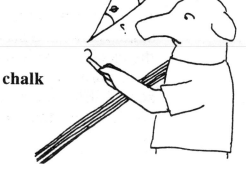

155   **cession**\SESH un\ n. handing over to another
session\SESH un\ n. a meeting of an assembly or court

156   **chalk**\CHOK\ n. a soft white or gray limestone
chock\CHOK\ adv. as full as possible
n. a wedge, a metal bar used for towing

chalk

157   **chance**\CHANS\ n. luck, opportunity,
ground for hope   v. to happen, to risk
chants\CHANtS\ n. hymns, monotone songs
v. sings

158 **chased**\CHAYST\ v. hunted, followed
chaste\CHAYST\ adj. innocent, pure

chased

chaste

159 **cheap**\CHEEP\ adj. at a low price   n. a bargain
cheep\CHEEP\ n. a peeping sound   v. to chirp

160 **check**\CHEK\ n. a bank draft   v. to inspect
Czech\CHEK\ n. a Czechoslovakian   adj. from Czechoslovakia

161 **chic**\SHEEK\ adj. stylish, fashionable   n. style
sheik\SHEEK\ n. an Arab chief, also **sheikh**, also \SHAK\

choir

162   **choir**\KWI er\n. a group of singers   v. to sing in a chorus
      quire\KWI er\ n.. 24 or 35 sheets of paper

163   **cholate**\KOHL ayt\ n. a salt of cholic acid
      collate\KOHL ayt\ v. to stack in order

choral  **coral**

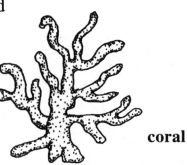

164   **choral**\KOR ul\ adj. having to do with a chorus or choir
      coral\KOR ul\ adj. bright pink
      n. the horny skeletal deposits made by polyps

165   **chorale**\kor AL\ n. a hymn, a chorus, also **choral**\kor AHL\
      corral\kor AL\ n. a pen for horses or other livestock

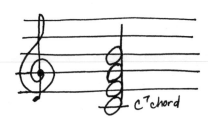

chord   **cord**

166   **chord**\KORD\ n. a combination of tones, a straight line
      joining two points on a curve, part of an airfoil   v. to harmonize
      cord\KORD\ n. a string or rope, a nerve, a unit of wood, a fabric
      with ribs   v. to tie up with cord, to pile up wood

shot

shoot

chute

167 **chott**\SHOT\ n. a North African dry salt lake bed, also **shott**
shot\SHOT\ n. a blast, an injection, a guess, one drink, one photo

168 **chou**\CHOU\ n. a fabric rosette, a cabbage
chow\CHOU\ n. food   v. to eat

169 **chute**\SHOOT\ n. a slide for a rapid descent, a parachute
shoot\SHOOT\ v. to fire a gun or let fly a missile, to wound or kill, to send a shuttle through threads, to move forward suddenly, to set off, to stick out, to take a picture, to grow up suddenly

cinque

170 **cinque**\SINgK\ n. five, also \SANgK\
sink\SINgK\ n. a pool for water, a basin
v. to go under, to decline
sank\SANgK\ v. submerged

sink

sank

171 **cis**\SIS\ adj. having certain atoms on the same side of a molecule
     sis\SIS\ n. sister
     siss\SIS\ v. to hiss

172 **cist**\SIST\ n. wicker chest to carry ancient Roman utensils in funerals
     cyst\SIST\ n. a closed sac, a spore
     sist\SIST\ n. a prehistoric grave

sight

cite

173 **cite**\SIT\ v. to summon, quote, or praise
     cyte\SIT\ n. a maturing germ cell
     sight\SIT\ adj. knowing without studying   n. act of seeing   v. to see
     site\SIT\ n. the position of a town, building, or monument
     v. to locate, to put into position

clack

174 clack\KLAK\ v. to chatter
n. continuous talk
claque\KLAK\ n. group hired to applaud

claque

175 clamber\KLAMb er\ v. to climb awkwardly
clamor\KLAM er\ v. to make loud noises,
also **clamour**

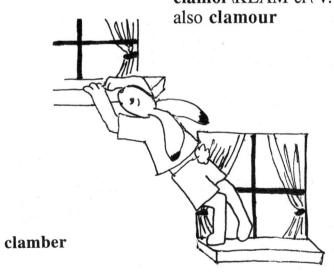

clamber

clamor

176 **Claus**\KLAHS\ n. Santa Claus
clause\KLAHS\ n. a group of words, a separate section of writing
claws\KLAHS\ n. sharp hooks on the ends of animal toes

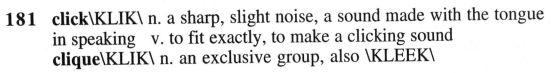

"...Far over the piled hills, and past
The hills she knew, she travelled fast;
She found a valley like a cup
With moonshine to the brim
filled up."
C.S. Lewis

177 **cleave**\KLEEV\ v. to divide in half, to glue
cleeve\KLEEV\ n. a cliff, a steep sloping hill often by a river

178 **cleek**\KLEEK\ n. a large hook for a pot over a fire
clique\KLEEK\ n. an exclusive group, also \KLIK\

179 **cleft**\KLEFT\ adj. partially divided   n. a space made by a split
klepht\KLEFT\ n. a Greek belonging to an armed, independent
community after the Turkish conquest, also **clepht**

180 **clew**\KLOO\ n. a ball of yarn, a metal loop on a sail, evidence,
lines of a hammock   v. to roll into a ball, to haul a sail up and down
clue\KLOO\ n. evidence

181 **click**\KLIK\ n. a sharp, slight noise, a sound made with the tongue
in speaking   v. to fit exactly, to make a clicking sound
clique\KLIK\ n. an exclusive group, also \KLEEK\

182 **climb**\KLIM\ n. the act of climbing   v. to go up or down, to grow over
clime\KLIM\ n. weather, climate

183 **close\KLOHS** adj. near
close\KLOHZ v. to shut
clothes\KLOHTHZ n. clothing

184 **coal\KOHL** n. a fossil fuel, a burning ember   v. to burn charcoal
cole\KOHL n. cabbage
kohl\KOHL n. black eyeliner

185 **coaming\KOHM ing** n. a raised frame around a ship's hatch
to keep out water
combing\KOHM ing v. grooming hair

186 **coarse\KORS** adj. rough texture, ordinary, inferior quality, crude talk
course\KORS n. a path from point to point, a subject, the area for playing golf,
a series of lectures   v. to hunt, to chase

coarse

course

187 **coat\KOHT** n. a covering
v. to cover with a protective layer
cote\KOHT n. a shed or coop

188 **coign**\KOIN\ n. cornerstone on a building, also **quoin**
coin\KOIN\ n. metal money   v. to make coins, to invent

189 **collie**\KAHL ee\ n. a Scottish sheepherding dog
colly\KAHL ee\ n. soot, grime

190 **colonel**\KERN ul\ n. an officer in the military
kernel\KERN ul\ n. a seed of grain, fruit or nut

191 **comb**\KOHM\ n. an instrument for grooming hair, the crest on a bird, a beehive   v. to arrange hair, to search carefully
combe\KOHM\ n. a deep, narrow valley

My how handsome Oscar has grown since I was here!

Please don't pinch my cheeks, Aunt Margaret.

192 **complement**\KOM pluh ment\ n. something that completes, accessories, the personnel on a ship, the other of two angles that equal 90 degrees, an interval of music, a part of blood, the opposite colors on a color wheel   v. to complete
compliment\KOM pluh ment\ n. a comment of respect or admiration

compliment

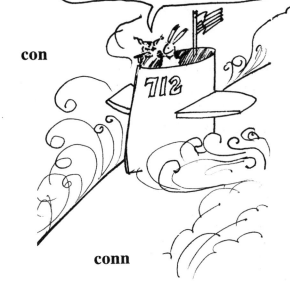

con

On one hand, we could dive. On the other hand, we could stay on the surface...

conn

193 **con**\KON\ adj. taking the opposing side   adv. in opposition
n. arguments against something, fraud
v. to memorize, to swindle
conn\KON\ n. the control of a ship's steering
v. to supervise the steering of a ship
khan\KON\ n. a medieval Chinese ruler,
central Asian ruler, a rest house, also \KAN\

194 **coo**\KOO\ n. sound of a pigeon   v. to make the sound
of a dove, to speak lovingly
coup\KOO\ n. a brilliant stroke, the sudden overthrow
of government

195 **cope**\KOHP\ n. a long vestment   v. to overcome problems, to notch
or fit to another piece, to cover with a vestment
coup\KOHP\ v. to overturn, to upset

196 **cops**\KOPS\ n. policemen   v. slang for to steal, to catch
copse\KOPS\ n. thicket, small woods

197 **core**\KOR\ n. the inedible central part of a fruit or vegetable,
the center   v. to take out the inedible center of a fruit or vegetable
corps\KOR\ n. a military unit, an association of German university students

198 **corespondent**\kor uh SPON dunt\ n. person sued for adultery
correspondent\kor uh SPON dunt\ n. person who exchanges letters

199 **council**\KOUN sul\ n. a group, an assembly
counsel\KOUN sul\ n. advice, a lawyer, a consultant   v. to advise

200 **cowrie**\KOU ree\ n. beautiful shelled mollusks used for ornaments or money, also **cowry, courie**
kauri\KOU ree\ n. a New Zealand pine tree, also **cawrie, kaurie, kawry, cowrie, kaori**

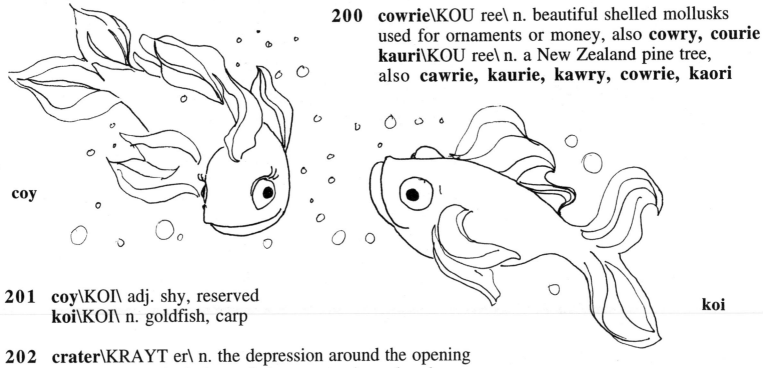

coy

koi

201 **coy**\KOI\ adj. shy, reserved
koi\KOI\ n. goldfish, carp

202 **crater**\KRAYT er\ n. the depression around the opening of a volcano, the hole made by a meteorite or bomb
krater\KRAYT er\ n. ancient black and orange Greek vase

203 **crawl**\KRAHL\ n. a swimming stroke   v. to creep slowly
krall\KRAHL\ n. an African village

204 creak\KREEK\ n. a grating noise   v. to make a grating noise
creek\KREEK\ n. a small stream, in Britain a cove or alley
Creek\KREEK\ n. a North American Indian tribe

205   crease\KREES\ n. a line made by folding   v. to fold, to wound slightly
kris\KREES\ n. Malay or Indonesian double-scalloped dagger,
also **kriss, creese**

206   croon\KROON\ v. to sing softly
kroon\KROON\ n. basic monetary unit of Estonia from 1928 to 1940

207   cue\KYOO\ n. a signal   v. to signal
queue\KYOO\ n. a long pigtail braid at the back of the head,
a line of people or vehicles

curr

cur

208   cur\KER\ n. a dog
curr\KER\ v. to coo, to make the murmuring sound of doves or pigeons

currant

current

209 **currant**\KER unt\ n. a small raisin
current\KER unt\ adj. the present time, commonly accepted
n. the swiftest part of a stream, electrical force, the flow of force

210 **curry**\KER ee\ n. food seasoned with curry powder
v. to brush with a currycomb, to beat or thrash, also **curie**
kerry\KER ee\ n. a short club used by South African aborigines,
a knobkerry

211 **cycle**\SI kul\ n. a repeated series of events,
one complete vibration, a bicycle   v. to recur
psychal\SI kul\ adj. relating to the mind

212 **dab**\DAB\ n. a touch, a pat, a flatfish
daub\DAB\ n. a smudge, something crudely applied
v. to plaster, coat, or apply crudely, also \DAHB\

213 **dam**\DAM\ n. a barrier holding back water   v. to put up a barrier
damn\DAM\ v. to curse, to condemn

214 **daughter**\DOT er\ n. female child
dodder\DOD er\ n. a leafless, parasitic herb
dotter\DOT er\ n. one who makes dots

215 **dawdle**\DOD ul\ v. to waste time
doddle\DOD ul\ v. to nod the head

dawn

Please, please... Let it be Saturday...

Call the men to don their armor! We ride into battle at dawn!

don

216 **dawn**\DON\ n. morning, the first light of morning   v. to realize
don\DON\ n. a Spanish noble, head of an Oxford or Cambridge college
v. to put on

217 day\DAY\ n. 24 hours, the time when the sun shines
dey\DAY\ n. a governor of Algeria before 1830

218 days\DAYZ\ adv. daily   n. plural for day
daze\DAYZ\ v. to confuse, to stun

219 deal\DEEL\ n. a large amount, an agreement
v. to pass out cards, to bargain, to trade
deil\DEEL\ n. the devil

220 dear\DEER\ adj. expensive, valued
deer\DEER\ n. hoofed mammal
whose males have antlers or horns

daze   days

221 deed\DEED\ n. contract, performance, something done
v. to transfer, a contract
deid\DEED\ adj. dead, also \DAD\

222 deem\DEEM\ v. to have the opinion, to judge
deme\DEEM\ n. a local community of related
organisms, a modern Greek commune

223 desert\DEZ ert\ n. land that receives
ten or fewer inches of annual rainfall
desert\du ZERT\ v. to leave without permission
n. just reward
dessert\du ZERT\ n. a sweet course of food

dessert

224 deuce\DOOS\ n. the face of a playing card or die
with two pips or spots
douce\DOOS\ adj. cheerful, tidy, respectable

225 **dew**\DYOO\ n. water condensed out of the air
do\DOO\ n. a festival, a battle   v. to bring about,
to produce, to play a part, to wash dishes
doux\DOO\ adj. very sweet, having at least 7% sugar
due\DYOO\ adj. owed, required, scheduled
adv. exactly (due north)   n. debt or fees

dye

226 **dey**\DI\ n. a Scottish dairymaid, also **deye**
die\DI\ n. a cube with dots, a tool that finishes
or shapes, a template, v. to pass away,
to stop working, to cut with a shaping tool
dye\DI\ n. coloring, pigment   v. to color

227 **dhak**\DOK\ n. a yellow dye
from an East Indian tree, also **dak**
dock\DOK\ n. a coarse weed, a wharf, the tail,
the place where the prisoner stands in court

228 **dhal**\DOL\ n. pigeon pen, also **dholl**
doll\DOL\ n. a toy person

die

229 **dhan**\DUN\ n. wealth in India determined by cattle
done\DUN\ adj. finished, cooked enough   v. finished
dun\DUN\ adj. color of a horse with a tan body
and black mane and tail   v. to pester for money

230 **dhikr**\DIK er\ n. the recitation of adoration of Allah
dicker\DIK er\ v. to bargain

231 **dhole**\DOHL\ n. a wild dog of India
dole\DOHL\ n. money or food given to the needy or unemployed, something alloted

232 **dhoon**\DOON\ n. a valley in India
dune\DOON\ n. a hill of sand

233 **dhuti**\DOOT ee\ n. a Hindu man's loincloth,
also **dhooti, dhoti**\DOH tee\
duty\DYOOT ee\ n. an action of respect or obligation,
a tax, active military service, the work of a machine

234 **dine**\DIN\ n. dinner v. to eat
dyne\DIN\ n. a unit of force

doe

dough

235 **dinkey**\DINK ee\ n. a small locomotive
dinky\DINK ee\ adj. small
dinghy\DING kee\ n. an East Indian rowboat
or sailboat, a ship's small boat

236 **discreet**\dis KREET\ adj. modest,
shows judgement in speech
discrete\dis KREET\ adj. separate
independent elements

237 **disease**\di ZEEZ\ n. a sickness
disseize\di SEEZ\ v. to be taken from
wrongfully, also **disseise**

238 **do**\DOH\ n. first tone of the diatonic scale
doe\DOH\ n. a female deer
dough\DOH\ n. a mixture of flour, water,
and other ingredients

239 **docile**\DOS ul\ adj. teachable, tame
dossal\DOS ul\ n. an ornamental cloth on the back of a throne, also **dossel, dorsal**

240   **docked**\DAHKT\ v. shortened, reduced, penalized,
brought into port, perforated (as a pie crust) before baking
dought\DAHKT\ v. recovered from an illness,
concerned enough to take action, past tense of **dow**

241   **dollar**\DOL er\ n. unit of American or Canadian money, a coin or bill
dolor\DOL er\ n. grief, sorrow, also **dolour** \DOL er\

242   **dollop**\DOL up\ n. a blob of whipped cream or ice cream, a small portion
v. to serve in dollops, to plop, also **dallop**
doll up\DOL UP\ v. to dress up in fancy clothes, to add decorative details

243   **dooly**\DOOL ee\ n. a litter carried on men's shoulders, also **doolie, dhooly**
dually\DYOO ul ee\ adv. in two ways
duly\DYOOL ee\ adv. in due time, eventually

244   **door**\DOR\ n. a swinging barrier, a gate
dor\DOR\ n. a beetle

245   **dot**\DOT\ n. a small spot, a period   v. a dowry, to mark with spots
dought\DOT\ v. form of dow, to be able to

246   **doubt**\DOUT\ n. a feeling of uncertainty   v. to distrust, to be undecided
dout\DOUT\ v. to put out, to extinguish, also \DOOT\

247   **doubter**\DOUT er\ n. a skeptic, an unbeliever, also \DOUD er\
douter\DOUT er\ n. a candlesnuffer, also \DOOT er\

248   **douc**\DOOK\ n. a variegated-colored monkey of Cochin, China
duke\DOOK\ n. ruler of a duchy, the highest English peer,
a raised fist as a symbol of victory, a cardplayer's hand

249 dour\DOU er\ adj. grumpy, gloomy, stubborn, also \DOO er\
dower\DOU er\ n. money or goods given with a bride,
the inheritance of a widow from her husband, money given for a bride

250 dries\DRIZ\ v. loses wetness
drys\DRIZ\ n. prohibitionists

251 droop\DROOP\ v. to hang down, to sink slowly
drupe\DROOP\ n. a one seeded fruit such as a cherry

252 dual\DYOO ul\ adj. having two parts
duel\DYOO ul\ n. a formal fight between two people

253 ducked\DUKT\ v. one's head lowered quickly
to avoid getting hit by something, dived below the water's surface
duct\DUKT\ n. a tube or channel   adj. a kind of tape

ducked

duct

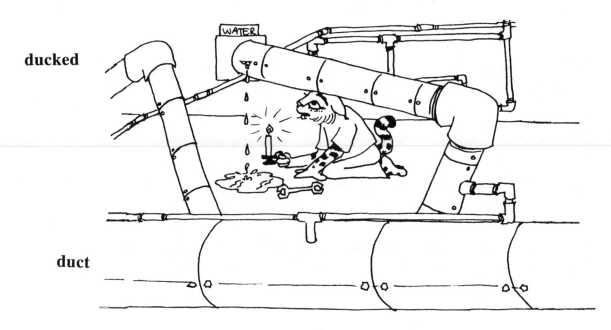

erne

earn

urn

254 **earn**\ERN\ v. to receive for work, to get, to grieve
erne\ERN\ n. an eagle, also **ern**
urn\ERN\ n. a vase

eaves

eves

255 **eaves**\EEVZ\ n. the part of a roof
that hangs out over the walls
eves\EEVZ\ n. evenings, the nights before

256 **ensure**\en SHUR\ v. to make certain,
to assure, to insure
insure\in SHUR\ v. to contract for insurance

257 **ewe**\YOO\ n. a female sheep
yew\YOO\ n. an evergreen tree or shrub
you\YOO\ pron. the one spoken to

faille

file

phial

258 **faille\FI ul** n. shiny silk, rayon or cotton cloth with slight ribs
file\FI ul n.. a flat ridged tool for smoothing surfaces,
a tool used to sharpen teeth on a saw, a box to store papers,
a row of squares on a chessboard   v. to smooth, to put papers in order,
to march in rows
phial\FI ul n. a vial

259 **fain\FAYN** adj. archaic for obliged, happy, willing
feign\FAYN v. to pretend

260 **faint**\FAYNT\ adj. feeling weak or dizzy
n. the act of fainting   v. to pass out
feint\FAYNT\ n. a distracting blow   v. to pretend

faint

feint

261 **fair**\FAIR\ adj. beautiful, clear weather, following the rules, blond,
weighing each side without prejudice   n. something beautiful,
a local market, an exhibit of food, art, or animals
fare\FAIR\ n. the price of a ticket, food   v. to get along, to eat

fair

fare

262 **fairy**\FAIR ee\ n. a tiny, magical, mythical person
ferry\FAIR ee\ n. a boat, a place where a river
is crossed by boat   v. to carry by boat

fairy

ferry

263 **farci**\FAR see\ adj. stuffed with oysters, also **farcie**
farcy\FAR see\ n. a disease of cattle

264 **fat**\FAT\ adj. overweight
phat\FAT\ adj. type-face that is easily and rapidly set
v. to keep type in the hope that there will be another order

265 **fate**\FAYT\ n. whatever happens was supposed
to happen, destiny   v. to doom
fete\FAYT\ n. a festival   v. to honor with a festival

266 **father**\FOTH er\.n. male parent, the originator
of an idea, leader   v. to sire, to start
fother\FOTH er\ n. wagonload, unit of weight for lead,
fodder   v. to cover a sail with oakum to stop a leak

faun

fawn

267 **faun**\FON\ n. a mythical Roman god with a human torso and head with a goat's body, beard, horns, etc.
fawn\FON\ n. a baby deer   v. to flatter, to gain approval

268 **fay**\FAY\ n. a fairy or elf
fey\FAY\ adj. doomed, able to see the future

phase

Why do they always fight when there is a full moon?

269 **faze**\FAYZ\ v. to upset
feeze\FAYZ\ n. a state of excitement, also \FEEZ\
phase\FAYZ\ n. a recurring stage of a cycle, to introduce a plan in stages

faze   **feeze**

feat

270 **feat**\FEET\ adj. an accomplishment, record setting deed, archaic for stylish
feet\FEET\ n. plural for foot

feet

271 **feel**\FEEL\ v. to touch
fjeld\FEEL\ n. a barren Scandinavian plateau, also \FYEL\

272 **felloe**\FEL oh\ n. curved rim of a spoked wheel, also **felly**
fellow\FEL oh\ n. boy or man, a friend, a peer, a member of a university, a paid graduate student

273 **felt**\FELT\ v. touched, sensed
veld\FELT\ n. grassland of southern Africa, also **veldt**

274 **fie**\FI\ interj. a cry of dismay
phi\FI\ n. the 21st letter of the Greek alphabet

275 **filum**\FIL um\ n. a filament
phylum\FIL um\ n. a primary group of animals, a group of languages

276 **fir**\FER\ n. a pine tree, an evergreen
fur\FER\ n. the hair on an animal, bacterial growth
on the tongue   v. to line with fur

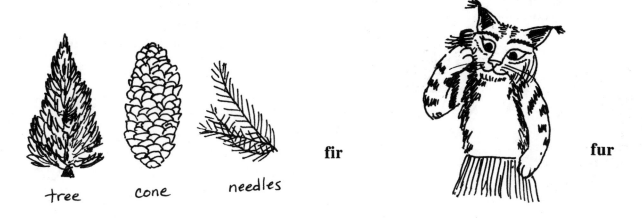

tree   cone   needles   **fir**   **fur**

277 **fizz**\FIZ\ n.. a hissing sound, a bubbly beverage   v. to make bubbles
phiz\FIZ\ n. face

278 **flair**\FLAYR\ n. a natural abiltiy   v. to hit with a stick, to thresh
flare\FLAYR\ n. a signal light, reflected light on a lens or photograph

279 **flay**\FLAY\ v. to skin, to harshly criticize
fley\FLAY\ v. to frighten, to startle

280 **flea**\FLEE\ n. a wingless bloodsucking insect
flee\FLEE\ v. to run away

flue

flu

This fire will keep you warm, Kenia.

281 **flech**\FLEK\ n. Scottish for flea
fleck\FLEK\ n. a spot, a flake

282 **fleury**\FLER ee\ adj. like a fleur de lis, a French lily
flurry\FLER ee\ n. a quick scattering of snow, a brief gust of wind

flew

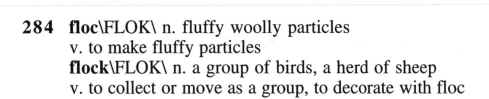

283 **flew**\FLOO\ v. soared, took to the air
flu\FLOO\ n. a virus, influenza
flue\FLOO\ n. a chimney

284 **floc**\FLOK\ n. fluffy woolly particles
v. to make fluffy particles
flock\FLOK\ n. a group of birds, a herd of sheep
v. to collect or move as a group, to decorate with floc

285 **flocks**\FLOKS\ n. groups of birds, herds
phlox\FLOKS\ n. annual or perennial herb with variegated flowers

286 **flour**\FLOU er\ n. finely ground grain
flower\FLOU er\ n. a blossom   v. to bloom

flour  **flower**

287 **for**\FOR\ prep. shows purpose, toward, because of, the equal to
fore\FOR\ adj. forward   n. front
interj. golfer's warning that a ball has been hit
four\FOR\ n. the number 4

288 **foreword**\FOR werd\ n. the introduction of a book
forward\FOR werd\ adj. toward the front, pushy, too familiar

289 **fort**\FORT\ n. a stronghold, a protected place
forte\FORT\ n. from the middle of the sword to its hilt,
the strongest part

290 **forth**\FORTH\ adv. moving forward, come out of
fourth\FORTH\ n. 4th

291 **foul**\FOUL\ adj. smelly, tangled, a ball out of bounds
n. breaking a rule   v. to break a rule
fowl\FOUL\ n. a bird

foul

fowl

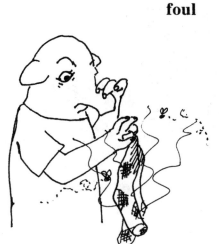

292 **frae**\FRAY\ prep. from
fray\FRAY\ n. a fight, an unraveled spot on cloth
v. to unravel

293 **fraise**\FRAYZ\ n. confusion, pointed stake obstacles,
a strawberry heraldic symbol   v. to ream out a hole, also **frase**
frays\FRAYZ\ v. unravels
phrase\FRAYZ\ n. an expression, sentence element,
a musical thought   v. to say in words

294 **franc**\FRANK\ n. French money
frank\FRANK\ adj. open and sincere, obvious   n. the signature
of someone sending free mail   v. to mail for free

295 **freedom**\FREE dum\ n. liberty
fretum\FREE dum\ n. a strait

296 freeze\FREEZ n. a cold state   v. to turn to ice, to stop moving

frieze\FREEZ n. a sculpture with a flat back often in the triangular space above columns on classical style buildings

frieze

freeze

297 friar\FRI er n. a religious brother

frier\FRI er** n. a young chicken, a pot for frying, also **fryer

friar

frier

298 fro\FROH\ adv. back again   prep. from
froe\FROH\ n. a tool for splitting shingles
frow\FROH\ v. to make barrels

299 furs\FERZ\ n. pelts, animal skins
furze\FERZ\ n. gorse, common European evergreen shrubs

300 gaff\GAF\ n. a hook, a spur on a gamecock, a cheap theater,
a steel pointed climbing iron used by telephone linepersons,
a spar for a sail, a hoax   v. to hit with a gaff, to fit a spur, to cheat
gaffe\GAF\ n. a social blunder

gage

gauge

301 gage\GAYJ\ n. a token of defiance, a deposit, a stake
gauge\GAYJ\ n. a tool for measuring or testing size,
the distance between train tracks, a gun barrel's diameter
v. to measure

302 **gain**\GAYN\ adj. straight, handy   n. profit   v. to get, to increase
gaine\GAYN\ n. a pillar supporting a sculptured bust

303 **gait**\GAYT\ n. way of moving, the walk, trot, and canter of horses
gate\GAYT\ n. a door, an opening, the total ticket sales
v. to control with a gate

304 **gallop**\GAL up\ n. the three beat gait of quadrapeds,
a run   v. to run fast, to canter
galop\GAL up\ n. a lively dance, also \gal OH\

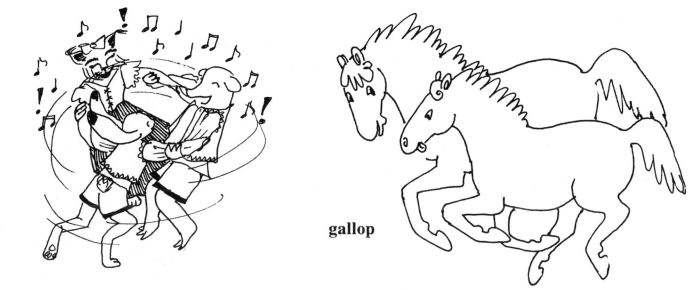

galop

gallop

305 **gam**\GAM\ n. a school of whales, conversation
between whalers at sea, slang for leg   v. to visit, to talk
gaum\GAM\ v. to smudge

306 **gamble**\GAM bul\ n. the act of taking a chance   v. to bet, to risk
gambol\GAM bul\ v. to frisk about

gamble

gambol

307 **gange**\GANJ\.v. to wrap with wire to protect a fishing hook or line
gangue\GANJ\ n. worthless rock in which valuable minerals are found, also **gang**\GANG\

308 **gaud**\GOD\ n. a trinket
god\GOD\ n. a person
or thing that is worshipped

309 **gay**\GAY\ adj. happy, lively,
homosexual
gey\GAY\ adv. very

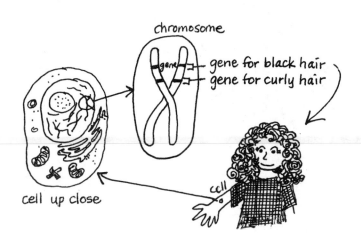

gene

jean

310 **gene**\JEEN\ n. the part of the cell containing the replicating code
jean\JEEN\ n. denim pants

311 **genet**\JEN ut\ n. animal related to the civet, skunk
jennet\JEN ut\ n. a female donkey,
a hinny: father a horse and mother a donkey

312 **gest**\JEST\.n. gesture, also **geste**
jest\JEST\.n. a funny remark, a joke   v. to joke

313 **ghat**\GOT\.n. stairs going into an Indian river, also \GAT\
got\GOT\.v. received, have

ghoul

gul

314 **ghoul**\GOOL\.n. an evil thing that robs graves and eats the dead
gul\GOOL\.n. a rose

315 **gild**\GILD\.v. to put on a thin layer of gold,
to give the appearance of great value
guild\GILD\.n. a group of craftsmen or merchants,
an interdependent ecosystem of plants

316 **gilt**\GILT\.adj. covered with gold, gold colored
n. gold or a thin layer of gold, a young female pig
guilt\GILT\ n. having broken a law

gilt

guilt

317 **gin**\GIN\ n. a trap, a machine for separating cotton seeds from fiber,
an alcoholic beverage
jinn\GIN\ n. a genie, also **jinni**\JIN ee\

318 **girl**\GERL\.n. a female child, a maid, sweetheart
gurl\GERL\ v. to howl, growl, Scottish for snarl

319 **girly**\GERL ee\ adj. featuring barely clothed girls, also **girlie**
gurly\GERL ee\ adj. stormy, surly, Scottish for gurgling

320 **girnie**\GERN ee\ adj. ill tempered
gurney\GERN ee\ n. a stretcher

321 **glair**\GLAIR\.n. egg white sizing, also **glaire**
glare\GLAIR\.n. an uncomfortably bright light, an angry stare
v. to shine a bright light, to stare

322 **gneiss**\NIS\.n. granite
nice\NIS\.adj. well behaved, pleasant

I'm also called a wildebeest.

gnu

Mom just got those new dishes, Sis, so try not to break any this time

I knew that!

knew

new

...Kκ, Λλ, Mμ, (Nν) Ξξ...

nu

323 **gnu**\NYOO\.n. an African antelope
knew\NYOO\.v. understood, to have had the information
new\NYOO\.adj. just made, a beginning
nu\NYOO\.n. 13th letter of the Greek alphabet

324 **grate**\GRAYT\.n. a frame of bars, a screen
great\GRAYT\.adj. a large amount, one generation removed, skilled

325 **grill**\GRIL\.n. a barbeque, a restaurant
v. to question, to broil
grille\GRIL\.n. ornamental screen on the front of a car

(Sigh.) This is going to take me forever!

great   **grate**

326 **grim**\GRIM\ adj. fierce, cruel, stern
grimme\GRIM\ n. a small, deep bay colored West African antelope

327 **grip**\GRIP\.n. a strong hold, a suitcase   v. to grab
grippe\GRIP\.n. flu, a viral infection

328 groan\GROHN\.v. to make a deep moaning sound
grown\GROHN\.adj. more developed   v. raised

guessed   **guest**

329 guessed\GEST\.v. approximated,
chose randomly
guest\GEST\.n. a visitor

330 **gyve**\JIV\.n. a shackle, a restraint
jive\JIV\.n. swing music, the talk of hipsters
v. to dance to swing music, to tease

331 **hackie**\HAK ee\.n. a cabdriver
hacky\HAK ee\ adj. hacking cough

332 **hae**\HAY\.v. to have
hay\HAY\.n. grass feed   v. to harvest and store hay
hey\HAY\.interj. a call of surprise, greeting, also **heigh**

hate

333 **haet**\HAYT\.n. a small amount
hate\HAYT\.n. feeling of intense dislike
due to fear, anger, or hurt
v. to strongly dislike

haet

334 **haik**\HIK\.n. an Arab's flowing white outer robe
hike\HIK\.n. a long walk, the act of lifting up   v. to lift up, to walk

335   **hail**\HAYL\.n. round lumps of ice   v. to rain down with great force
            hale\HAYL\.adj. healthy   v. to haul

hair

"Rapunzel, Rapunzel, let down your hair."

hail

hare

hale

336   **hair**\HAIR\.n. threadlike growth on mammals
            hare\HAIR\.n. animal like a rabbit

have

halve

337 **haler**\HOL er\.n. 1/100 of a Czech koruna
holler\HOL er\.n. a shout, a small valley
v. to yell

338 **hall**\HOL\.n. a corridor, a castle,
a college building, an auditorium
haul\HOL\.v. to pull, to carry,
to change course

339 **halve**\HAV\.v. to cut into two pieces
have\HAV\.n. a rich person   v. to get, to own, to eat, to beget

340 **handsome**\HANT sum\.adj. a large amount, good looking
hansom\HANT sum\.n. a small 2-wheeled horse drawn carriage

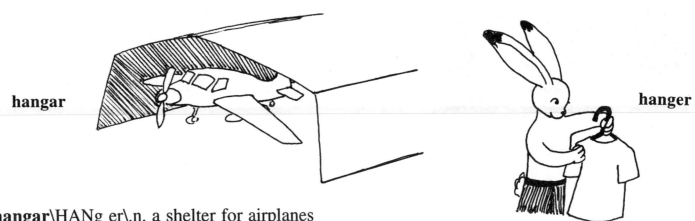

hangar

hanger

341 **hangar**\HANg er\.n. a shelter for airplanes
hanger\HANg er\.n. a loop or bar to hang clothes

342 **harl\HARL** n. a tangled mass   v. to drag an object on the ground
harle\HARL** n. flax or hemp stalk, also **herl

343 **hart\HART\.** n. a mature male red deer
heart\HART\. n. organ that pumps blood, courage, a playing card,
the most important part

hawk

hock

344 **haugh\HOK\.** n. a meadow by a stream
hawk\HOK\. n. a bird of prey, a falcon   v. to hunt with a hawk
hock\HOK\. n. a joint in a horse's hind leg, a joint in a fowl's leg

345 heal\HEEL\.v. to cure, to return to health
heel\HEEL\.n. the back of the foot,
the ends of a bread loaf, the base
of something, a rotten person
he'll\HEEL\.he will, he shall

heal

heel

he'll

346 healer\HEEL er\.n. person who cures, a Christian Science practitioner
heeler\HEEL er\.n. local political party worker,
one who stays by your side

347   **hear**\HEER\ v. to listen, to consider testimony
here\HEER\.adv. at this place
interj. an answer at roll call   n. this place

hear

here

348   **heard**\HERD\.v. listened, learned
herd\HERD\ n. group of animals, a mob
v. to move animals

he'd

349   **he'd**\HEED\ he had, he would
heed\HEED\ n. a notice
v. to pay attention

350 **heigh**\HI\ interj. call of surprise or question
hi\HI\ interj. hello
hie\HI\ v. to hurry
high\HI\ adj. something above, tall, of great rank, superior, feeling
elated, drunk, expensive   adv. at a high position   n. a hill,
a transmission gear, high barometric pressure

351 **height**\HIT\ n. the elevation,
the vertical measurement
hight\HIT\ adj. called, named

352 **heroin**\HAIR oh wun\ n. narcotic more potent than morphine
heroine\HAIR oh wun\ n. lead female character

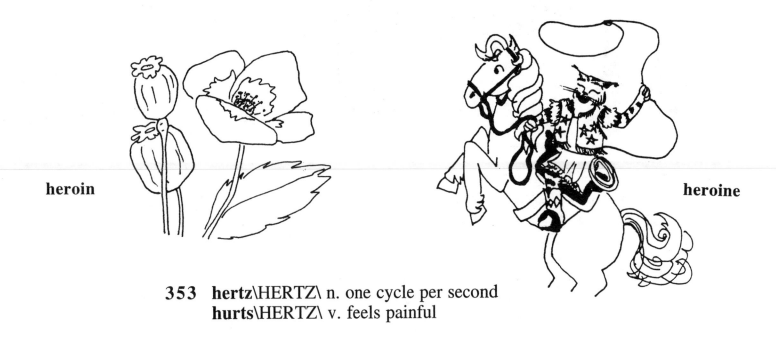

heroin   heroine

353 **hertz**\HERTZ\ n. one cycle per second
hurts\HERTZ\ v. feels painful

354 **hew**\HYOO\ v. to cut, to stick to the rules
hue\HYOO\ n. color

355 **higher**\HI er\ adj. above
hire\HI er\ n. wages or payment
v. to employ someone

higher

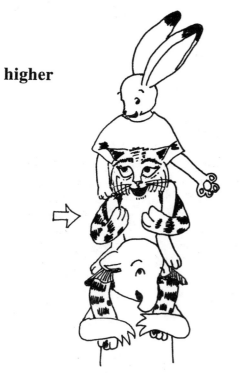

hire

356 **him**\HIM\ pron. objective case of he
hymn\HIM\ n. a religious song

357 **ho**\HOH\interj. cry to get someone's attention
hoe\HOH\ n. tool to cut weeds   v. to scrape weeds, etc.
whoa\HOH\ v. command to a draft animal to stop, also \WOH\

358 **hoar**\HOR\ n. frost
hor\HOR\ adj. horizon
whore\HOR\ n. a prostitute

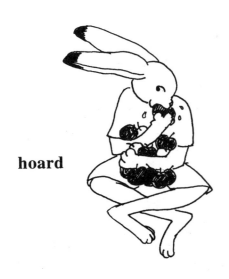

hoard

horde

359 **hoard**\HORD\ n. a hidden supply
v. to hide supplies
horde\HORD\ n. a mob,
a tribal group of Mongolian nomads

360 **hoarse**\HORS\ adj. having a gruff
voice or sore throat
horse\HORS\ n. large one-toed
mammal used for riding and
carrying   v. to get mounted and ride

361 **hoes**\HOHZ\ v. weeding tools
hose\HOHZ\ n. stockings,
a long flexible tube
for conducting water
v. to wash or spray
with a hose

362 **hole**\HOHL\ n. an opening,
a burrow, a hovel
whole\HOHL\ adj. complete,
healed   n. total

hose

hoes

363 **holey**\HOHL ee\ n. something with holes
holi\HOHL ee\ n. Hindu spring festival
holy\HOHL ee\ adj. sacred, worshipped
wholly\HOHL ee\ adv. completely

364 **holm**\HOHM\ n. a small inshore island, low land by a river or stream
home\HOHM\ n. house, dwelling, the object in many games
v. to send to a destination

365 **hooch**\HOOCH\ n. illegal alcoholic liquor
hootch\HOOCH\ n. a thatched hut in southeast Asia

366 **hornie**\HORN ee\ n. the devil
horny\HORN ee\ adj. made of horn

hostel

Welcome to the Sleepyhead Inn

hostile

367 **hostel**\HAHST ul\ n. an inn
hostile\HAHST ul\ adj. unfriendly

368 **hour**\OU er\ n. the time
our\OU er\ pron. belongs to us

369 **how**\HOU\ adv. why   conj. the way or condition   n. questioning
howe\HOU\ n. valley

370 **humerus**\HYOOM er us\ n. the long bone from the shoulder to elbow
humorous\HYOOM er us\ adj. funny, amusing

371 **I'd**\ID\ I had, I should, I would
ide\ID\ n. edible freshwater fish of Europe

idyll

Ah...to live a simple life at one with Nature— I'd give my kingdom for a simple life!

SIMPLE COUNTRY LIFE ON THE NILE

Lazy, good for nothing...

idle

idol

372 **idle**\ID ul\ v. to do nothing, to run an engine in neutral
idol\ID ul\ n. a worshipped object
idyll\ID ul\ n. a writing about the simple country life,
a romantic interlude, also **idyl**

373 **impatience**\im PAY shunts\ n. feeling restless, irritated by waiting
impatiens\im PAY shunts\ n. a flower

374 **in**\IN\ prep. into, within
inn\IN\ n. a hotel

375 **indict**\in DIT\ v. to charge with a crime
indite\in DIT\ v. to write, to make up

376 **its**\ITS\ adj. belongs to it
it's\ITS\ it is, it has

377 **jam**\JAM\ n. a crowded condition,
a fruit preserve   v. to stop movement,
to overfill, to make radar or radio signals
unreadable, to play music
in an unstructured session
jamb\JAM\ n. a door frame

jam

jamb

378 **jewel**\JYOO ul\ n. a precious stone
joule\JYOO ul\ n. a unit of work or energy

379 **kain**\KIN\ n. a sarong
kine\KIN\ n. archaic plural for cow

380 **kayak**\KI ak\ n. an Eskimo canoe
kyack\KI ak\ n. a pack hung on either side of a saddle

381 kill\KIL n. the object killed, place names of creeks in Delaware and New York   v. to take the life, to destroy, to smash a ball so hard that it cannot be returned
kiln\KIL n. an oven, also \KILN\

382 kite\KIT n. a hawk, a light covered frame flown in the wind   v. to soar, to write a check without enough money in the bank to cover it
kyte\KIT n. stomach

383 knap\NAP n. crest of a hill   v. to snap off pieces with a quick blow
nap\NAP n. a short sleep, the way a woven surface lies   v. to take a short sleep especially during the day

need

Are you almost done with that bowl, 'cause I'll need it soon.

Just a sec

kneed

BANG! KITCHEN

384 knave\NAV n. a male servant, a rascal
nave\NAV n. the main part of a church, wheel hub

385 knead\NEED v. to shape by pressing together repeatedly
kneed\NEED v. struck with the knee
need\NEED n. a necessity, lacking necessities v. to require, to lack

386 knee\NEE n. a leg joint   v. to strike with the knee
nee\NEE adj. a woman's maiden name, also \NAY\

387 knight\NIT n. a mounted, feudal warrior v. to make into a knight
night\NIT n. the period from dusk to dawn, evening

388 **knit**\NIT\ v. to interlock yarn, to grow together
nit\NIT\ n. a louse egg

389 **knob**\NOB\ n. door opening device
nob\NOB\ n. cribbage point, one in a higher class in Britain

390 **knobby**\NOB ee\ adj. lumpy
nobby\NOB ee\ adj. chic, smart

391 **knock**\NOK\ n. a pounding sound   v. to strike with force, to criticize
nock\NOK\ n. the notches on either end of a bow that hold the string

knot

naught

not

392 **knot**\NOT\ n. tied or tangled loops of string,
a measure of a ship's speed, a sandpiper,   v. to tie
naught\NOT\ adj. insignificant   n. nothing, zero
not\NOT\ adv. gives words the opposite meaning

393 **knotty**\NOT ee\ adj. complex, full of knots
naughty\NOT ee\ adj. bad, disobedient

394 **knout**\NOOT\\NOUT\ n. a flogging whip
newt\NYOOT\ n. a salamander

395 **know**\NOH\ v. to understand, to have the required skill, to recognize
no\NOH\ adj. not any   adv. the opposite of yes

nose

noes

396 **knows**\NOHZ\ v. understands, remembers
noes\NOHZ\ plural of no
nose\NOHZ\ n. the part of the face that breathes and smells
v. to scent, to detect, to rub with the nose

397 **krona**\KROHN uh\ n. basic monetary unit of Iceland
krone\KROHN uh\ n. Austrian money from 1892-1925

398 **la**\LAH\ n. 6th tone of the diatonic scale
law\LAH\ n. a rule, the legal profession

399 **laager**\LAHG er\ n. a protected camp
surrounded by wagons or armed vehicles
lager\LAHG er\ n. beer
logger\LAHG er\ n. one who cuts trees for a living

400 **lac**\LAK\ n. a form of shellac secreted by scale insects
lack\LAK\ n. the state of being in need   v. to have missing
lakh\LAK\ n. 100,000, Indian for a great number, also \LOK\

lei

lay

401 **lade**\LAYD\ v. to load a burden
laid\LAYD\ v. set down, deposited an egg

402 **lai**\LAY\ n. a medieval French tale often about Arthur and
the Round Table, a lyric poem revived in the 17th century
laigh\LAY\ adj. low
lay\LAY\ n. a share in a whaling ship's profit,
the angle of threads in cloth   v. to put down,
to deposit an egg, to spread over
lea\LAY\ n. grassland, also **ley**
lei\LAY\ n. Hawaiian necklace of flowers

lane

403 **lain**\LAYN\ v. reclined
lane\LAYN\ n. a path between fences, a shipping route, a lined course for cars, runners, etc.

404   **lakh**\LOK\ n. a great number
       loch\LOK\ n. a lake, a nearly landlocked bay
       lock\LOK\ n. hairs, a door security device, a system
       for raising and lowering water in a canal, a wrestling hold   v. to secure
       lough\LOK\ n. a lake, a bay

405 **lam**\LAM\ n. running away from the law
v. to hit, to run away
lamb\LAM\ n. a young sheep   v. to have a lamb

406 **lama**\LAH muh\ n. a Buddhist monk
llama\LAH muh\ n. a South American ruminant
without a hump similar to a camel, also \YAH muh\

407 **laps**\LAPS\ v. licks, covers, overtakes
lapse\LAPS\ n. a mistake, the end of a limit   v. to run out of time,
to forfeit

408 **lat**\LOT\ n. Latvian money from 1922-1940
lot\LOT\ n. a share, one's fate, a parcel of land   v. to divide portions

409 **lea**\LEE\ n. meadow, also **ley**
lee\LEE\ n.. quarter toward which the wind blows
li\LEE\ n. a Chinese distance about 1/3 mile

410 **leach**\LEECH\ n. a strainer for wood ashes while extracting lye
leech\LEECH\ n. a bloodsucking worm, a vertical edge of a square sail
v. to bleed with a leech

411 **lead**\LED\ n. a soft gray metal, bullets
led\LED\ v. directed, to be first

412 **leaf**\LEEF\ n. plant foliage,
a movable section of a table,
a sheet of paper   v. to grow leaves,
to page through a book
lief\LEEF\ adj. beloved
adv. willingly, also \LEEV\

leaf

413 **leak**\LEEK\ n. a hole that lets something out
v. to drip out, to escape
leek\LEEK\ n. an herb in the lily family
like a mild green onion

lief

414 **lean**\LEEN\ n. having no fat   v. to tip to one side
lien\LEEN\ n. a legal claim on property as security for a debt

415 **leased**\LEEST\ v. rented
least\LEEST\ adj. the smallest

416 **leaven**\LEV un\ n. yeast   v. to raise bread
levin\LEV un\ n. lightning

417 **less**\LES\ adj. fewer, smaller, lower rank
loess\LES\ n. loamy dirt deposited by wind

418 **lessen**\LES un\ v. to decrease, to reduce
lesson\LES un\ n. a unit of teaching   v. to lecture

419 **liar**\LI er\ n. one who does not tell the truth
lier\LI er\ n. one who lies in ambush
lyre\LI er\ n. a Greek stringed instrument

420 **lie**\LI\ n. the position of something,
the haunt of an animal
v. to recline, to deceive
lye\LI\ n. an alkaline substance
leached from wood ashes

421 **lief**\LEEV\ adj. beloved
leave\LEEV\ n. permission
v. to bequeath, to not take with you

422 **lieu**\LOO\ n. instead
loo\LOO\ n. a card game,
in England a toilet   v. to have
to chip in for a new game

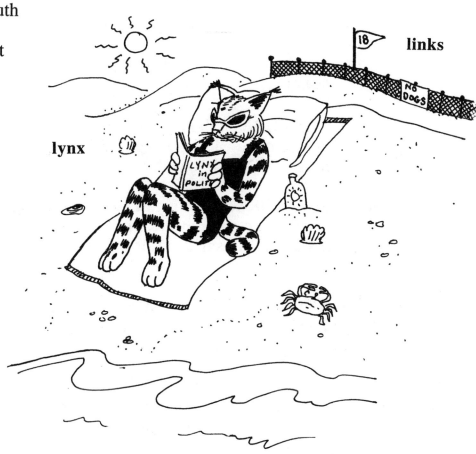

links

lynx

423 **links**\LINKS\ n. sand hills near the seashore, a golf course
lynx\LINKS\ n. bobcat, a short tailed mottle-coated wildcat

424 lo\LOH\ interj. cry of surprise or to get attention
low\LOH\ adj. below, under, cheap   n. lowest gear,
area of low barometric pressure
lowe\LOH\ n. a flame or blaze

425 load\LOHD\ n. a burden, a cargo   v. to put on or in
lode\LOHD\ n. a deposit of ore within other rock

426 loan\LOHN\ n. borrowed money   v. form of to lend,
to give out money and expect that money back plus interest
lone\LOHN\ adj. one, by itself

427 locks\LOKS\ n. system of gates for raising and lowering
water in a canal, devices with keys   v. secures
lox\LOKS\ n. smoked salmon

428 loop\LOOP\ n. a doubling of line, a handle, a ring
loupe\LOOP\ n. a small magnifying glass used by jewelers

429 loot\LOOT\ n. stolen goods   v. to destroy and steal
lute\LOOT\ n. a stringed musical instrument,
a coating to keep out a gas or liquid
v. to seal with lute

430 lope\LOHP\ n. a slow canter   v. to canter
loup\LOHP\ v. to leap, to flee

431 lory\LOR ee\ n. a parrot, a lorikeet of Australia
lorry\LOR ee\ n. a truck

maid   **made**

432 **ma**\MAH\ n. mama, an obsolete musical tone
maw\MAH\ n. jaws, stomach, an opening,
a seagull, also **maa**

433 **made**\MAYD\ adj. invented, artificially produced
v. caused to happen, cooked, shaped
maid\MAYD\ n. a young unmarried girl

434 **mail**\MAYL\ n. letters, the postal service,
armor   v. to send letters
male\MAYL\ adj. and n. refering
to the sex that fertilizes, man

435 **mailer**\MAYL er\ n. an envelope for mailing,
one who mails
maler\MAYL er\ n. males

436 **main**\MAYN\ adj. most important   n. chief part, water or gas pipe
mane\MAYN\ n. thick hair growth on horse's neck and male lions

437 **mair**\MAIR\ adv. more
mare\MAIR\ n. female horse

438 **maize**\MAYZ\ n. Indian corn
maze\MAYZ\ n. puzzle of many paths   v. to perplex, to bewilder

439 **mall**\MAHL\ n. a large group of stores, a game, a pedestrian walkway
maul\MAHL\ n. a large heavy hammer   v. to beat, to split wood
moll\MAHL\ n. a gangster's girlfriend

manor

manner

440   **manner**\MAN er\ n. custom, sort, kind
         manor\MAN er\ n. estate, mansion

441 mantel\MAN tul n. shelf over a fireplace
mantle\MAN tul n. a cloak

442 marc\MARK n. debris from pressed fruit
mark\MARK n. a sign, target, victim, scratch,
a unit of old European money
marque\MARK n. a brand name, permission from a government
to capture enemy merchant ships

443 marlin\MAR lun n. a sailfish, swordfish
marline\MAR lun n. a two strand rope wound around a ship's rope

444 marry\MAIR ee v. to wed, to join, to perform a wedding
merry\MAIR ee adj. happy, cheerful

445 marshal\MARSH ul n. sheriff,
head of the cavalry of a medieval king
martial\MARSH ul adj. military

446 marten\MAR tun n. a weasel
martin\MAR tun n. a swallow

mask

masque

447 mask\MASK n. a cover for the face
v. to disguise, to cover
masque\MASK n. a short drama
of the 16th and 17th centuries

448 **massed**\MAST\ v. collected, formed
mast\MAST\ n. a long pole on which to hang a sail

449 **mat**\MAT\ n. a floor covering, pad, a border for a picture
v. to press together, to put a border on a picture
matte\MAT\ adj. a dull finish   n. a mixture of sulfides

450 **mawk**\MAWK\ n. a maggot
mock\MAWK\ adj. fake, imitation   n. a sneer,
a stump or root   v. to defy, to imitate, to ridicule

451 **me**\MEE\ pron. the objective case of I
mi\MEE\ n. the third tone of the diatonic scale

452 **mead**\MEED\ n. a meadow, an alcoholic drink
made from honey, malt, and yeast
meed\MEED\ n. a reward

453 **mean**\MEEN\ adj. low in rank, humble, despicable
n. average   v. to have in mind
mesne\MEEN\ adj. intervening, middle

454 **meat**\MEET\n. food, flesh
meet\MEET\ v. to join, to find
mete\MEET\ v. to hand out, to assign

455 **medal**\MED ul\ n. a circular metal disk used as a prize
meddle\MED ul\ v. to interfere

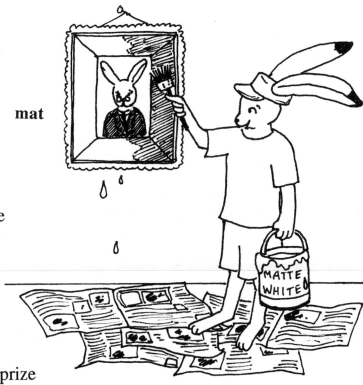

mat

matte

mind

456 **mer**\MER\ n. a unit of polymer
murre\MER\ n. a razorbill seabird
myrrh\MER\ n. an aromic gum resin

457 **metal**\MET ul\ n. hard, shiny substances such as gold or silver
mettle\MET ul\ n. character

458 **mewl**\MYOOL\ n. a whimper, meow   v. to whimper
mule\MYOOL\ n. the offspring of a donkey father and horse mother

459 **might**\MIT\ n. power   v. possibly could, probably would
mite\MIT\ n. a tiny spider, a small coin

460 **mil**\MIL\ n. a unit of length 1/1000 of an inch
mill\MIL\ n. a building or machine
for grinding grain, a machine for making coins, polishing
stones, etc.   v. to grind, to mix

461 **milch**\MILK\ adj. bred for producing milk
milk\MILK\ n. liquid from mammary glands
of female mammals for feeding their young
v. to draw milk from teat or udder

mined

462 **mind**\MIND\ n. brain, memory, opinion
v. to obey, to notice
mined\MIND\ v. dug out ore

463 **miner**\MIN er\ n. a person who digs for ore
minor\MIN er\ adj. less important, not serious   n. a person 17 years or younger
v. to take courses in a second area of emphasis

464 **minks**\MINKS\ n. weasel-like animals valued for their pelts
minx\MINKS\ n. a vivacious perky girl

465 **missal**\MIS ul\ n. a hymnal, prayerbook
missile\MIS ul\ n. a rocket, a bullet

466 **missed**\MIST\ v. failed to hit, noticed the absence of
mist\MIST\ n. a light rain, a cloud over the eyes

467 **mixed**\MIKST\ v. combined
mixt\MIKST\ n. a mixture, a compound

moan

Oh...my aching back.,

468 **moan**\MOHN\ v. to complain
mown\MOHN\ v. cut, shaped

469 **moat**\MOHT\ n. the ditch around a castle
mote\MOHT\ n. a speck

470 **mold**\MOHLD\ n. a fungus
mown
mould\MOHLD\ n. the top of the head,
the incomplete closing of a fetal or young skull

471 **moo**\MOO\ n. the lowing sound of a cow
moue\MOO\ n. a pout
mu\MOO\ n. the 12th letter of the Greek alphabet

472 **moor**\MOR\ n. open rolling barren land   v. to anchor
mor\MOR\ n. forest humus
more\MOR\ adj. greater, additional amount

473 **moose**\MOOS\ n. a large North American mammal with huge antlers
mousse\MOOS\ n. a spongy food, foamy hair gel

474 **morn**\MORN\ n. dawn, daybreak
mourn\MORN\ v. to grieve

475 **morning**\MORN ing\ adj. during the first part of the day
n. the time from dawn to noon
mourning\MORN ing\ n. the custom of showing grief, the black
clothing and other symbols of death

476 **mow**\MOH\ v. to cut
mowe\MOH\ v. to grimace

477 **murra**\MER uh\ n. semi-precious stone
or porcelain used to make ancient Roman vessels
murrah\MER uh\ n. an Indian buffalo

478 **mus**\MUS\ n. a house mouse
muss\MUS\ v. to wrinkle, to make untidy

479 **naval**\NAYV ul\ adj. having to do
with ships or warships
navel\NAYV ul\ n. the bellybutton, middle

480 **nay**\NAY\ adv. no
neigh\NAY\ n. a horse's cry
v. to make the cry of a horse

481 **nicks**\NIKS\ n. notches, chips
nix\NIKS\ adv. no   n. a Germanic folklore
female watersprite that is half human, half fish

482 **nil**\NIL\ n. nothing, zero
nill\NIL\ v. to refuse

483 **none**\NUN\ adv. in no way   pron. no one,
no part   n. fifth of the canonical hours
nun\NUN\ n. a woman who has taken vows of chastity,
humility, and poverty

484 **o**\OH\ n. zero, the letter O
oh\OH\ interj. call of surprise, pain, or pleasure
owe\OH\ v. to need to pay, to be in debt

485 **oak**\OHK\ n. a hardwood tree with acorns
oke\OHK\ n. a unit of weight in Turkey, Greece,
and Egypt of about 2.8 pounds

486 oar\OR\ n. a paddle
   o'er\OR\ prep. over
   or\OR\ conj. either, alternative
   ore\OR\ n. mineral containing metal

ore

o'er

or

oar

Should I go after that guy or stay here with this gold?

Goldie

487 od\OD\ n. the natural power underlying hypnotism
   odd\OD\ adj. strange

488 ode\OHD\ n. a poem
   owed\OHD\ v. indebted

489 one\WUN\ adj. a single thing   pron. any person   n. the number 1
   won\WUN\ v. succeeded, was the first

490 pa\PAH\ n. father
   pas\PAH\ n. a dance step, the right of precedence
   paw\PAH\ n. foot   v. to strike the ground with a hoof, to feel or grope

491 paced\PAYST\ v. trotted, walked back and forth
   paste\PAYST\ n. a glue, a flour dough, imitation jewels   v. to glue

492 **packed**\PAKT\ adj. ready to travel
v. filled, loaded
pact\PAKT\ n. a treaty

493 **pail**\PAYL\ n. a bucket
pale\PAYL\ adj. light colored

Sorry I can't play, coach. My arm hurts!

pain

pane

494 **pain**\PAYN\ n. physical
or mental suffering, an unpleasant feeling
pane\PAYN\ n. a section of window glass

pare

pear   **pair**

495 **pair**\PAIR\ n. a couple, two things meant to be together
pare\PAIR\ v. to shave or trim
pear\PAIR\ n. a fruit

496 **palate**\PAL ut\ n. the roof of the mouth, taste
palet\PAL ut\ n. the chaffy scale on plants
palette\PAL ut\ n. a board for holding paint,
a set of colors
pallet\PAL ut\ n. a mattress, a platform for cargo
pallette\PAL ut\ n. a plate of armor at the armpits

497 **pall**\PAHL\ n. a cloak   v. to cover with a cloak
pawl\PAHL\ n.. a tongue in a ratchet wheel

498 **pallor**\PAL er\ n. lacking color, paleness
parlor\PAH ler\ n. sitting room, a business such as a beauty parlor

499 **par**\PAR\ n. common level, number of strokes allotted per golf hole
parr\PAR\ n. young fish especially salmon in fresh water

500 **passed**\PAST\ v. successfully completed a course or test, went by or through
past\PAST\ adj. happened before now   prep. after
n. an earlier occurrence

501 **pate**\pah TAY\ n. a spiced mashed meat
pattee\puh TAY\ n. a heraldic cross

502 **pate**\PAHT\ n. pottery slip for making porcelain
pot\PAHT\ n. a kettle

pause

Shh... wait here a second.

Ow! Use your paws not your claws!

503 **pause**\PAHS\ n. a wait
paws\PAHS\ n. animal feet
v. impatiently strikes the ground
with a hoof

paws

504 **pax**\PAHKS\ n. peace
pocks\PAHKS\ n. holes

505 **pay**\PAY\ v. to exchange goods or services for money   n. wages
pe\PAY\ n. 17th letter of the Hebrew alphabet

506 **pea**\PEE\ n. a seed of a leguminous vine
pee\PEE\ n. the letter p

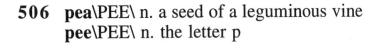

pea

507 **peace**\PEES\ n. stillness, the state of tranquility
piece\PEES\ n. part of the whole, a work of art, a gun, a chessman

508 **peak**\PEEK\ n. mountain top, highest point   v. to reach the maximum
peek\PEEK\ v. to look through a crack, to glance
pique\PEEK\ n. a fit of resentment   v. to annoy, to excite

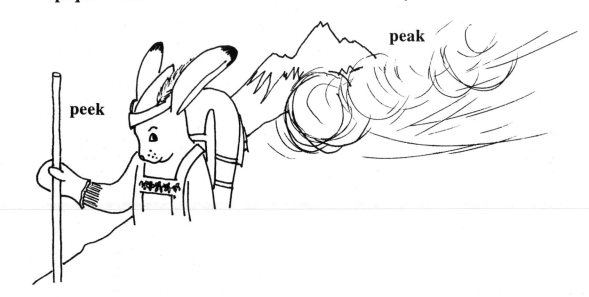

peak

peek

509 **peal**\PEEL\ n. the sound of a bell   v. to toll a bell
peel\PEEL\ n. the outer skin of fruit or vegetable   v. to remove skin

510 **pearl**\PERL\ n. a growth in oysters used as a gemstone
purl\PERL\ n. gold thread edging, the gentle swirling of a stream v. to gently swirl, to knit

purl   pearl

511 **peas**\PEEZ\ n. seeds of a leguminous vine
pes\PEEZ\ n. the foot, the tenor in a medieval choir

512 **peer**\PEER\ n. a colleague, one of the five ranks of British nobles
pier\PEER\ n. a wharf, a support under a floor or bridge

513 **pend**\PEND\ n. a Scottish arch or passageway v. to depend
penned\PEND\ v. wrote, corralled

514 **penni**\PEN ee\ n. 1/100 of a Finnish markka
penny\PEN ee\ n. 1/100 of a U.S. or Canadian dollar

515 **per**\PER\ prep. for each, through, by means of
purr\PER\ n. the low vibrating sound of a happy cat

516 **petit**\PET ee\\puh TEET\ adj. archaic for secondary
petite\puh TEET\ adj. small   n. clothing size for short women
petty\PET ee\ adj. small minded, mean, lower rank

517 **pi**\PI\ n. the ratio of the circumference to the diameter
of a circle which equals about 3.14, the 16th letter in the Greek alphabet
pie\PI\ n. a pastry filled with fruit or meat, a magpie,
a multicolored animal, former Indian money equal 1/192 of a rupee

picul

pickle

518 **pial**\PI ul\ adj. relating to the brain and spinal cord
pile\PI ul\ n. a heap, a steel or wooden pole,
a hemorrhoid v. to stack

519 **pickle**\PIK ul\ n. a vegetable preserved in salt
and vinegar   v. to preserve in a brine of salt and vinegar
picul\PIK ul\ n. a Chinese and Southeast Asian
unit of weight equal to about 133.33 pounds

520 **picks**\PIKS\ n. pointed tools   v. pecks, chooses
pyx\PIKS\ n. a vessel to carry the Eucharist to the sick,
also **pix**   v. to test a coin for weight and fineness

521 **pique**\pi KAY\ n. ribbed fabric
piquet\pi KAY\ n. a two-handed card game with 32 cards

522 **pistil**\PIST ul\ n. the ovary organ of a seed plant
pistol\PIST ul\ n. a handgun

523 **pixie**\PIKS ee\ n. a fairy, a mischievious sprite, also **pixy**
pyxie\PIKS ee\ n. an evergreen shrub related to heaths

place

plaice

524 **place**\PLAYS\ n. space, area   v. to put
plaice\PLAYS\ n. a large European flounder

525 **plack**\PLAK\ adj. paltry   n. a small Scottish
coin issued from James III to James IV
plaque\PLAK\ n. an ornamented or painted plate, deposits on teeth

526 **plain**\PLAYN\ adj. undecorated, ordinary, obvious
adv. in an uncomplicated way   n. treeless country
plane\PLAYN\ n. a smoothing tool, a level surface,
an airplane   v. to level

527 **plait**\PLAYT\ n. a braid   v. to braid
plate\PLAYT\ n. a smooth metal sheet, a flat circular food dish,
a base in baseball, a full page illustration, dentures, a sheet of material
v. to cover with a layer

poler   polar

528   **polar**\POHL er\ adj. relating to the north or south poles, opposite
        poler\POHL er\ n. one who pushes a boat with a pole

529   **pole**\POHL\ n. a long stick, the inside position on a racetrack,
        the magnetized end
        poll\POHL\ n. the back of the head, the end of a hammer,
        a questioning of people at random for their opinion about something
        v. to receive and count votes, to cut off

530 pomace\PUM us\ n. the residue from crushed fruit
pumice\PUM us\ n. volcanic rock, the powder form of volcanic rock
v. to smooth with pumice

531 pool\POOL\ n. a small body of water, a pocket in sedimentary rock,
a game like billiards, a collection   v. to contribute to a fund
pul\POOL\ n. Afghani money

532 pore\POR\ n. a tiny opening in the skin or membrane
pour\POR\ v. to flow, to rain hard

533 praise\PRAYZ\ v. to commend, to worship
prase\PRAYZ\ n. a waxlike green quartz
prays\PRAYZ\ v. entreats, talks to God
preys\PRAYZ\ v. hunts

534 prau\PROU\ n. an Indonesian boat
prow\PROU\ n. the bow of a ship or airplane

535 pray\PRAY\ v. to plead, to talk to God
prey\PRAY\ n. an animal taken as food   v. to raid, to grab and eat

prayer

preyer

536 prayer\PRAY er\ n. one who pleads
preyer\PRAY er\ n. one who attacks

537 presser\PRES er\ n. person or thing that squeezes or presses
pressor\PRES er\ adj. raising or tending to raise blood pressure

pride   **pried**

538 **pride**\PRID\ n. the quality of being proud, having high self esteem
pried\PRID\ v. pulled out with a lever, opened with difficulty

539 **prier**\PRI er\ n. one who uses a lever to move something
prior\PRI er\ adj. earlier   n. a superior house or rank in a monastary

540 **pries**\PRIZ\ v. moves with a lever
prize\PRIZ\ adj. outstanding   n. an award   v. to value highly, also **prise**

541 **principal**\PRINS uh pul\ n. head of a school, the star performer
principle\PRINS uh pul\ n. a law, a main quality

542 **profit**\PROF ut\ n. the gain after expenses   v. to benefit
prophet\PROF ut\ n. a messenger from God

543 **psalter**\SAHL ter\ n. a book of sacred poems
salter\SAHL ter\ n. one who sells salt,
one who salts meat

544 **puisne**\PYOON ee\ adj. lower rank
puny\PYOON ee\ adj. weak,
less important

puny

puisne

545 **puli**\PUL ee\ n. a Hungarian dog
pulley\PUL ee\ n. a grooved wheel with ropes
that increases the force for lifting

546 **pursy**\PUS ee\ adj. fat, short winded
because of being overweight
pussy\PUS ee\ adj. full of pus

547 **qua**\KWAY\ prep. as
quay\KWAY\ n. a wharf for loading and unloading ships, also \KEE\

548 **qua**\KWAH\ n. a European night heron   prep. in the role of
quaw\KWAH\ n. a quagmire

549 **quad**\KWAHD\ n. a four sided enclosure, one of four
quod\KWAHD\ n. a prison

quarts

quartz

550 **quaich**\KWAYK\ n. a cup with ears for handles, also **quaigh**
quake\KWAYK\ n. an earthquake   v. to shake

551 **quarts**\KWORTZ\ n. more than one quart which is 1/4 of a gallon
quartz\KWORTZ\ n. the mineral silicone dioxide

552 **quean**\KWEEN\ n. an unmarried woman, a prostitute
queen\KWEEN\ n. wife of a king, female chief, a fertile female bee

553 **quitter**\KWIT er\ n. one who gives up easily
quittor\KWIT er\ n. an inflammation in horses' feet

554 **rabat**\RAB ut\ n. a polishing material made from fired clay
rabbet\RAB ut\ n. the groove in tongue and groove planks
rabbit\RAB ut\ n. a mammal similar to a hare

555 **race**\RAS\ n. a contest of speed, a strong current, a nation
v. to run in a contest, to run out of control, to rev an engine
res\RAS\ n. a particular thing especially in a legal phrase, also \REEZ\

556 **rack**\RAK\ n. a frame, an instrument of torture, neckbones of mutton
v. to torture, to move at the four beat gait of a Saddlebred horse
wrack\RAK\ n. seaweed, wind driven clouds, a wreck   v. to wreck

557 **racket**\RAK ut\ n. a lot of noise, an illegal business,
a light bat or paddle   v. to have an active social life, to make a lot of noise
racquet\RAK ut\ n. a gazelle

558 **racks**\RAKS\ n. bins, frames   v. strains
rax\RAKS\ v. to make long, to stretch
wracks\RAKS\ v. wrecks

559 **radical**\RAD uh kul\ adj. relating to the root
n. an advocate of extreme change, a basic principle
radicle\RAD uh kul\ n. the beginnings of the intestines or lungs

560 **raid**\RAYD\ n. a surprise attack   v. to pillage
rayed\RAYD\ adj. having flowers in a star pattern, having rays

561 **raik**\RAYK\ n. ground over which animals wander
rake\RAYK\ n. a toothed gardening and farming tool

562 **rail**\RAYL\ adj. relating to railroads
n. a bar on a fence, a wading bird
v. to scold, to make fun of, to fence
rale\RAYL\ n. the abnormal sound
of air passing through mucous

563 **rain**\RAYN\ n. water droplets
from clouds   v. to precipitate
reign\RAYN\ n. the period
of a ruler's authority   v. to rule
rein\RAYN\ n. one of the lines
on a bridle or harness

564 **raise**\RAYZ\ v. to grow, to set up,
to establish radio contact, to stir up
rase\RAYZ\ v. to erase
rays\RAYZ\ n. lines from a central point
raze\RAYZ\ v. to tear down

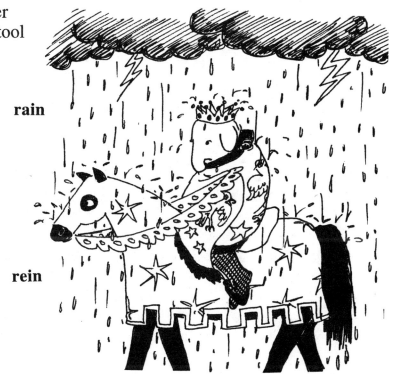

rain

rein

reign

565 **ranch**\RANCH\ n. a farm
ranche\RANCH\ n. a stroke in pin pool that wins the game

566 **rap**\RAP\ adj. a type of music   v. to criticize, to be carried upward
wrap\RAP\ v. to cover

567 **rapped**\RAPT\ v. knocked
rapt\RAPT\ adj. lifted by supernatural force,
totally absorbed   v. to be carried away by force
wrapped\RAPT\ v. covered, packaged, also **wrapt**

568 **raser**\RAYZ er\ n. one that erases, carves or engraves
razor\RAYZ er\ n. a cutting blade   v. to shave

569 **rathe**\RAYTH\ adv. early in the day
or season, also **rath**\RATH\
wraith\RAYTH\ n. a watersprite, a ghost

570 **rathe**\RATH\ adj. ready before the others
wrath\RATH\ adj. full of rage   n. violent anger

571 **ray**\RAY\ n. a fish, a line of light, an arrow
re\RAY\ n. the 2nd tone of the diatonic scale

572 **re**\REE\ prep. regarding, also \RAY\
ree\REE\ adj. irrational   v. to sift
ri\REE\ n. a Japanese unit of distance of about 2.44 miles

573 **reach**\REECH\ v. to stretch
reech\REECH\ n. smoke   v. to stink

ray

re ♪

574 **read**\RED\ v. to have studied and understood words
red\RED\ adj. the color or blood   n. a loss as in the red
redd\RED\ n. the spawning ground of fishes   v. to tidy

575 **read**\REED\v. to study, to understand words
rede\REED\ n. a story   v. to explain
reed\REED\ n. tall grasses, a family of musical instruments

read

rede

reed

576 **real**\REEL\ adj. land, genuine   adv. very, also **really**
reel\REEL\ n. a round spool for winding thread   n. a Scottish Highland dance
v. to twirl, to dance

577 **ream**\REEM\ n. 472, 480, or 500 sheets of paper   v. to widen an opening
riem\REEM\ n. a pliable strip of leather

578 **reave**\REEV\ v. to seize, to burst
reeve\REEV\ n. a local agent of an Anglo Saxon king, a local official, a female perch
v. to pass a rope through a hole and tie
reive\REEV\ v. to raid

579 reck\REK\ v. to worry about
wreck\REK\ v. to ruin

580 reek\REEK\ v. to stink
wreak\REEK\ v. to punish,
to get even

581 resail\REE sayl\ v. to sail again
resale\REE sayl\ adj.
sold a second time

582 rest\REST\ n. sleep, not moving,
silence in music, a stand   v. to sleep,
to end the presentation of evidence
wrest\REST\ n. the act of taking by force
v. to pull, to take by force

wreak   reek

Let's not do anything hasty, Chuck...

583 retch\RECH\ v. to vomit
wretch\RECH\ n. a pitiful person

584 revere\ruh VEER\ v. to worship
revers\ruh VEER\ n. a lapel on women's clothing

585 review\ruh VYOO\ n. a military inspection, a survey   v. to examine
revue\ruh VYOO\ n. a theatrical show of songs and skits

The fields clean and covered with rime,
Where once trees their leaves had cast,
Were sleepy with the wintertime;
Autumn was almost past.

rhyme   **rime**

586 **rex**\REKS\ n. a plush coated rabbit breed
wrecks\REKS\ v. ruins

587 **rheum**\ROOM\ n. tears
room\ROOM\ n. space, lodging, a walled part of a house

588 **rheumy**\ROOM ee\ adj. tearful
roomy\ROOM ee\ adj. spacious

589 **rho**\ROH\ n. 17th letter of the Greek alphabet
ro\ROH\ n. an artificial language that rejects words
roe\ROH\ n. a female deer, fish eggs
row\ROH\ n. a number of objects in lines
v. to move a boat with oars

590 **rhyme**\RIM\ n. words that end with the same sounds
rime\RIM\ n. frost, crust   v. to cover with frost

591 **right**\RIT\ adj. correct   adv. exactly   n. the law or custom
rite\RIT\ n. a ceremony
wright\RIT\ n. a carpenter
write\RIT\ v. to form letters, to spell, to compose

592 **ring**\RING\ n. a bell's sound, a circular band, a gang v. to sound a bell
wring\RING\ v. to squeeze and twist

593 **ringer**\RING er\ n. a competitor pretending to be someone else,
one who sounds a bell
wringer\RING er\ n. a machine that squeezes water from clothes

594 **riot**\RI ut\ n. a civil disturbance, a wild mob
ryot\RI ut\ n.. a Hindu soil cultivator

595 **road**\ROHD\ n. a street
rode\ROHD\ v. carried in or on
rowed\ROHD\ v. paddled a boat with oars

596 **roc**\ROK\ n. a huge legendary bird from the Indian Ocean area
rock\ROK\ n. a stone   v. to move back and forth

597 **roil**\ROY ul\ v. to stir up, to arouse
royal\ROY ul\ adj. related to the king,
magnificent, a mature stag
n. a small sail above the top gallant,
paper 20"x25" or 19"x24"

598 **role**\ROHL\ n. a part played
roll\ROHL\ n. a list of names, a scroll,
a yeast cake, folded money,
the sound of a drum, a somersault
v. to turn over and over, to rob
a sleeping person, to spread out

599 **roo**\ROO\ n. a kangaroo
roux\ROO\ n. a cooked mixture
of flour and fat
rue\ROO\ n. regret,
a medicinal herb   v. to regret

"No, truly, Ursula she is too distainful;
I know her spirits are as coy and wild
As haggards of the rock."

"But are you sure that Benedick
loves Beatrice so entirely?"

(from
Shakespeare's
"Much Ado About
Nothing")

role

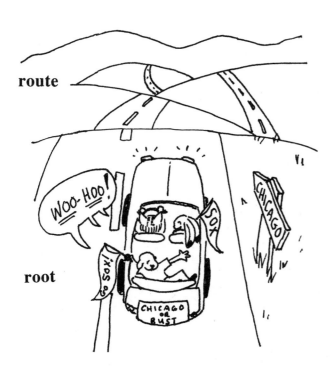

route

root

600 **rood**\ROOD\ n. a crucifix, 1/4 of an acre
rude\ROOD\ adj. offensive, primitive

601 **roose**\ROOZ\ v. to praise
roux\ROOZ\ n. cooked flour and fat mixtures
ruse\ROOZ\ n. a trick

602 **root**\ROOT\ n. the underground part of a plant, base,
source   v. to dig up, to develop, to cheer for one's team
route\ROOT\ n. direction, highway

603 **rope**\ROHP\ n. strong cord   v. to lasso
roup\ROHP\ n. an auction, to sell at auction

604 **rose**\ROHZ\ n. a fragrant flower with thorny stems
rows\ROHZ\ n. orderly lines   v. paddles a boat

605 **rot**\ROT\ v. to decay
wrought\ROT\ adj. made, finished, excited by, deeply stirred

606 **rote**\ROHT\ n. a repetition, the noise of surf on the shore
wrote\ROHT\ v. spelled, corresponded, composed

607 **rough**\RUF\ adj. uneven, coarse, difficult   n. tall grass,
a tough person, a first draft, an outline   v. to beat up, to outline
ruff\RUF\ n. a wheel shaped collar, fringe of feathers or fur,
the act of trumping a card   v. to trump

608 **rout**\ROUT\ n. a wild retreat, a reception, a fuss   v. to defeat soundly
route\ROUT\ n. a direction, a highway   v. to send

609 **ruelle**\ROO ul\ n. a narrow alley, a fashionalble French woman's
morning reception in the 17th and 18th centuries
rule\ROO ul\ n. a regulation, a law, a standard   v. to control

610 **rung**\RUNG\ n. crosspiece on a ladder, wheel spokes   v. sounded a bell
wrung\RUNG\ v. squeezed and twisted

611 **rye**\RI\ n. a cereal grass, a gypsy gentleman
wry\RI\ adj. crooked, ironic humor   v. to twist

612 **sac**\SAK\ n. a fluid filled pouch within a plant or animal
sack\SAK\ n. a bag, a woman's dress, a wine, also **sacque**
sacque\SAK\ n. a baby's jacket or gown

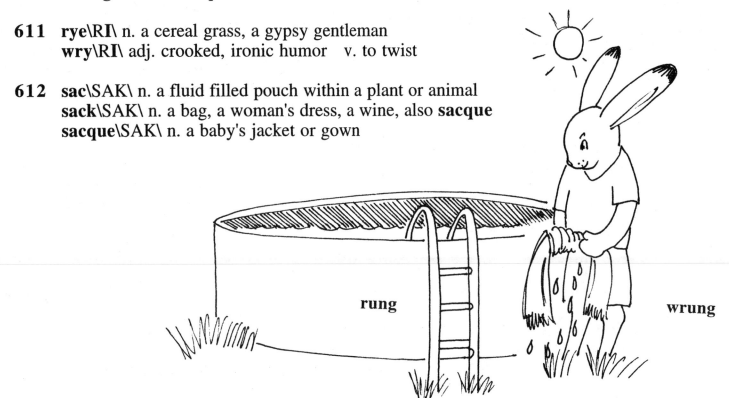

rung

wrung

sail

613   **sail**\SAYL\ n. canvas on a sailing ship that catches the wind,
a cruise   v. to travel by boat, to move easily
sale\SAYL\ n. the transfer of ownership of something,
an offering at a reduced price, an auction, the gross receipts

614   **sailer**\SAYL er\ n. a ship with certain sailing characteristics
sailor\SAYL er\ n. a crew member on a ship, a seaman

615   **sain**\SAYN\ n. the sign of the cross
sane\SAYN\ adj. mentally healthy
seine\SAYN\ n. a fishing net

616 salse\SAHLTS\ n. a mud volcano
salts\SAHLTS\ n. mineral mixture, Epsom salts v. seasons

617 sambar\SAHMB er\ n. a large Asiatic deer, also **sambur**
somber\SAHMB er\ adj. serious, gloomy

618 sari\SAH ree\ n. a long cloth worn by a Hindu woman
saury\SAH ree\ n. needlefish
sorry\SAH ree\ adj. feeling regret or pity

619 sauce\SAHS\ n. a relish, a dressing   v. to add zest, to be rude
soss\SAHS\ adv. heavily   n. mess, slop   v. to fall heavily

620 sauch\SAHK\ adj. sallow, pale, also **saugh**
sock\SAHK\ n. a knitted foot covering   v. to hit

621 scat\SKAT\ n. jazz singing   v. to scoot away, to make up syllables
scatt\SKAT\ n. a tax
skat\SKAT\ n. a three handed card game, also \SKOT\

622 scend\SEND\ n. the lift of a wave   v. to rise up on a wave
send\SEND\ v. to go, to order, to deliver

623 **scene**\SEEN\ n. part of a play, a location, bad manners in public
seen\SEEN\ v. have looked, have observed
sin\SEEN\ the 21st letter of the Hebrew alphabet

624 **scop**\SKOHP\ n. an old English poet
scope\SKOHP\ n. range, space for operating   v. a viewing instrument

625 **scot**\SKAHT\ n. a tax, an assessment
skat\SKAHT\ n. a three handed card game

626 **scrooge**\SKROOJ\ n. a miserly person
scrouge\SKROOJ\ v. to crowd, also **scruj**

627 **scull**\SKUL\ n. an oar or pair of oars,
a racing boat
v. to use an oar or pair of oars
skull\SKUL\ n. head bone

628 **scye**\SI\ n. the shape of an armhole, armscye
sigh\SI\ v. to release a big breath, to grieve

seem

seam

seam

629 **seam**\SEEM\ n. the stitching that holds two pieces
of cloth together, the space between planks on a ship,
a layer of ore between different strata of rocks   v. to stitch together
seem\SEEM\ v. to appear

630 **seaman**\SEEM un\ n. crewman on a boat, a sailor
semen\SEEM un\ n. male reproductive fluid containing sperm

631 **season**\SEEZ un\ n. a period of time, a part of the year, salt or spices
v. to add salt or spices, to treat lumber
seisin\SEEZ un\ n. the ownership of land,
also **seizin**

632 **senate**\SEN ut\ n. the second chamber
of a bicameral legislature,
ancient Roman supreme council,
a governing body
sennet\SEN ut\ n. a trumpet call
for stage entrances and exits
sennit\SEN ut\ n. braided cord,
straw, or fabric

sennet

sennit

senate

633 **serf**\SERF\ n. lowest feudal class
surf\SERF\ n. breaking waves on the shore
v. to ride a surfboard

634 **serge**\SERJ\ n.. a twilled fabric with noticeable diagonal lines
surge\SERJ\ n. the swelling of a wave, a sudden rise in electrical current
v. to rise and fall, to rise abnormally high

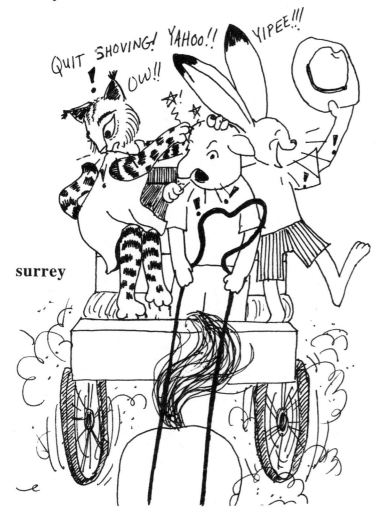

surrey

635 **serry**\SER ee\ v. to crowd together
surrey\SER ee\ n. a two-seated
horse drawn carriage

636 **sew**\SOH\ v. to stitch together
so\SOH\ adj. true   conj therefore
pron. the same
sow\SOH\ v. to plant seeds

637 **sewer**\SOO er\ n. a waterpipe
suer\SOO er\ n. one who takes someone to
court

638 **sewn**\SOHN\ v. has been stitched together
sone\SOHN\ n. the loudness 40 decibels
higher than the listener's threshold
for detecting sound
sown\SOHN\ v. to have planted seeds

639 **shake**\SHAYK\ n. a trembling, a milkshake,
a slat of wood used for roofing
v. to vigorously
move up and down or back and forth
sheik\SHAYK\ n. an Arab chieftain,
also **sheikh**\SHEEK\

640 **shear**\SHEER\ n. large scissors, a sliding of rock along a fracture   v. to cut hair
sheer\SHEER\ adj. transparent, vertical, perpendicular

641   **shiel**\SHEE ul\ n. a shepherd's mountain hut
she'll\SHEE ul\ she will, she shall

642   **shier**\SHI er\ n. a horse that startles easily, also **shyer**
shire\SHI er\ n. an English county, a breed of heavy draft horses

643   **shirr**\SHER\ v. to gather cloth, to bake shelled eggs
sure\SHER\ adj. certain, reliable   adv. certainly

shoo

644   **shoe**\SHOO\ n. footwear
v. to put metal plates
on horse hooves
shoo\SHOO\ v. to scare away

645   **shone**\SHOHN\ v. stood out from the rest,
to have had a light shine
shown\SHOHN\ v. to have demonstrated,
exhibited, or presented

646   **sic**\SIK\ adv. indicates the preceding words
are an exact copy of a misspelled word, such, very
v. to tell a dog to attack
sick\SIK\ adj. ill, tired, disgusted

shoe

647   **sighs**\SIZ\ v. releases a big breath, grieves
size\SIZ\ n. commonly accepted measurements, varnish, sealant
v. to arrange from small to large, to compare, to seal a surface

648 sign\SIN\ n. message, signal   v. to write one's name
sine\SIN\ n. a trigonometric function

649 Sioux\SOO\ n. North American plains Indian tribe
sou\SOO\ n. five cent French coin
sue\SOO\ v. to seek justice in a court, to woo

650 slay\SLAY\ v. to kill
sleigh\SLAY\ n. a vehicle with runners to slide on snow   v. to ride in a sleigh

651 sleave\SLEEV\ n. thread, a skein of yarn   v. to separate into threads
sleeve\SLEEV\ n. the part of clothes covering the arm, a hollow tube

652 sleight\SLIT\ n. craftiness, trickiness
slight\SLIT\ adj. weak, small   n. an insult   v. to ignore, to insult

653 slew\SLOO\ n. a large number   v. killed
slough\SLOO\ n. swamp, inlet of a river   v. to plow through mud
slue\SLOO\ n. the position after twisting   v. to veer, to spin around

654 sloe\SLOH\ n. blackthorn fruit
slow\SLOH\ adj. low speed, behind time, stupid
adv. slowly   v. to reduce speed

655 soak\SOHK\ n. the act of saturating   v. to submerge in liquid
sok\SOHK\ n. the right to hold court under early English law

656 soar\SOR\ n. upward flight   v. to fly, to glide
sore\SOR\ adj. painful, injured, angry   n. a wound, an infected spot

657 **soared**\SORD\ v. flew
sword\SORD\ n. a combat weapon
with a long, flat blade

658 **sol**\SOHL\ n. 5th tone of the diatonic scale
sole\SOHL\ n. undersurface of a foot or shoe
v. to put on a sole
soul\SOHL\ n. spirit, leader, moral force

659 **some**\SUM\ adj. a group   adv. somewhat
pron. an indefinite amount
sum\SUM\ n. the total from adding numbers,
the whole amount

660 **son**\SUN\ n. a male child
sun\SUN\ n. the Earth's star   v. to lie in the sun
sunn\SUN\ n. an East Indian plant
with fibers like jute and hemp

661 **sonny**\SUN ee\ n. a young boy
sunny\SUN ee\ adj. merry, exposed to sunlight

662 **soot**\SOOT\ n. fine powder left over from smoke
suit\SOOT\ n. a court action, a set of clothes,
all cards of the same pip, all same numbered dominoes
v. to dress, to be appropriate

663 **souter**\SOOT er\ n. a shoemaker
suitor\SOOT er\ n. one who petitions, a man courting a woman

664 **spade**\SPAYD\ n. a small shovel, a playing card
with the symbol of a small, pointed shovel
spayed\SPAYD\ v. to have removed the ovaries of a female animal

665 **spae**\SPAY\ v. to foretell the future
spay\SPAY\ v. to remove the ovaries of a female

666 **speel**\SPEEL\ v. to climb
spiel\SPEEL\ n. salesman's pitch   v. to talk constantly, to play music

667 **speiss**\SPIS\ n. a mixture of arsenic with other metals
spice\SPIS\ n. various seasonings such as pepper, nutmeg, etc.

668 **spoor**\SPOR\ n. the track of a wild animal   v. to follow animal tracks
spore\SPOR\ n. a reproductive cell of plants like mushrooms

669 **stade**\STAYD\ n. stadium
staid\STAYD\ adj. serious, sedate
stayed\STAYD\ v. remained behind

670 **staff**\STAF\ n. a long stick, employees, officers, a plaster wallcovering
staph\STAF\ n. staphylococcus

671 **stair**\STAIR\ n. steps
stare\STAIR\ v. to look without blinking, to focus attention

672 **stake**\STAYK\ n. a post, money, a share in a business
steak\STAYK\ n. a slice of meat or fish

673 stalk\STAHK\ n. stem of a plant   v. to follow, to hunt, to walk stiffly
stock\STAHK\ adj. standard   adv. completely   n. livestock, pillory, supplies, base of a gun or fishing pole   v. to supply, to load up

674 stalking\STAHK ing\ v. walking stiffly, hunting stealthily
stocking\STAHK ing\ n. a knitted foot and leg covering, a sock, markings on the lower legs of animals

675 stater\STAYT er\ n. an ancient Greek coin
stator\STAYT er\ n. the part of a machine that does not move

676 stationary\STAY shun air ee\ adj. in one place, not moving
stationery\STAY shun air ee\ adj. relating to writing materials
n. writing paper

677 steal\STEEL\ v. to take illegally
steel\STEEL\ adj. made of steel   n. an alloy of iron   v. to brace
stele\STEEL\ n. the wooden shaft of an arrow

678 stealer\STEEL er\ n. one who takes illegally
stelar\STEEL er\ adj. relating to the central part of a vascular plant, relating to the wooden shaft of an arrow

679 steer\STEER\ n. a castrated beef animal
stere\STEER\ n. one cubic meter

680 step\STEP\ n. stair, a foot movement   v. to walk, to dance
steppe\STEP\ n. a treeless tract of land in Eurasia

681 sterile\STAIR ul\ adj. barren, free from germs
sterol\STAIR ul\ n. cholesterol

682 stile\STIL\ n. turnstile, gate in a fence
style\STIL\ n. a custom, a pen, a bristle   v. to follow current fashion

683 stolen\STOHL un\ v. to have taken something illegally
stolon\STOHL un\ n. a branch that develops buds or runners

684 stoop\STOOP\ n. porch   v. to bend over
stoup\STOOP\ n. tankard, basin for holy water

685 straight\STRAYT\ n. a line, a perfect score, five cards in sequence
strait\STRAYT\ adj. close fitting, difficult   n. narrow body of water

686 straighten\STRAYT en\ v. to make straight
straiten\STRAYT en\ v. to squeeze together, to be in distress

687 **streak**\STREEK\ n. a bolt of lightning, a narrow band of light
v. to make a line, to run naked
streek\STREEK\ v. to lay out a dead body

688 **strider**\STRID er\ n. one who takes long steps
stridor\STRID er\ n. the harsh sound of obstructed expelled air,
a loud creaking noise

styler

Like it, dearie?
It's the latest
style!

stylar

689 **stylar**\STIL er\ adj. resembling a bristle
styler\STIL er\ n. one who designs hair, etc.

690 **succor**\SUK er\ n. help, relief
sucker\SUK er\ n. a fish, something that sucks,
a shoot from the root of a plant,
a person easily tricked, a lollipop

691 **suite**\SWEET\ n. an apartment, a group of rooms,
a musical score
sweet\SWEET\ adj. sugary, fragrant, pleasing
n. candy, dessert

tea

692 **sundae**\SUN day\ n. ice cream topped
with syrup, nuts, or fruit
Sunday\SUN day\ n. the first day of the week

693 **t**\TEE\ n. 20th letter of the English alphabet
tea\TEE\ n. leaves used to brew a drink
tee\TEE\ n. a peg for setting a golf ball,
a frame for setting a football
for kicking   v. to put a ball on a tee
ti\TEE\ n. 7th note of the diatonic scale

694 **tacks**\TAKS\ n. short nails
v. attaches, to change the direction
of a sailing ship
tax\TAKS\ n. money collected by a governing body
v. to charge, to make demands

695 **tael**\TAYL\ n. a Chinese unit of value based on silver
tail\TAYL\ n. the rear of an animal or airplane,
full evening dress for men, the reverse of a coin, a spy following someone
v.to attach to the end, to follow
tale\TAYL\ n. a story

696   **tailer**\TAYL er\ n. a shadow, one who follows
tailor\TAYL er\ n. one who makes or alters clothes
v. to make or alter clothes

tailer

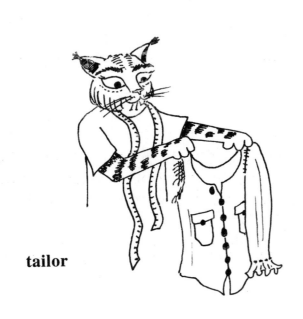

tailor

697   **taler**\TAHL er\ n. a silver German coin
taller\TAHL er\ adj. higher

698   **talk**\TOK\ n. speech   v. to speak
tock\TOK\ n. an African hornbill

699   **talker**\TOK er\ n. one who speaks
tocher\TOK er\ n. Scottish marriage portion, a dower
v. to provide with a marriage portion

700 **taper**\TAYP er\ adj. gradually narrowed to a point
n. a candle, something that dispenses tape
v. to diminish slowly
tapir\TAYP er\ n. a nocturnal ungulate
of tropical America, Malaya, and Sumatra
related to horses and rhinos

701 **tare**\TAIR\ n. vetch seed,
weight of the empty vehicle
v. to weigh the empty vehicle
tear\TAIR\ n. a hole, a split
v. to rip, to divide

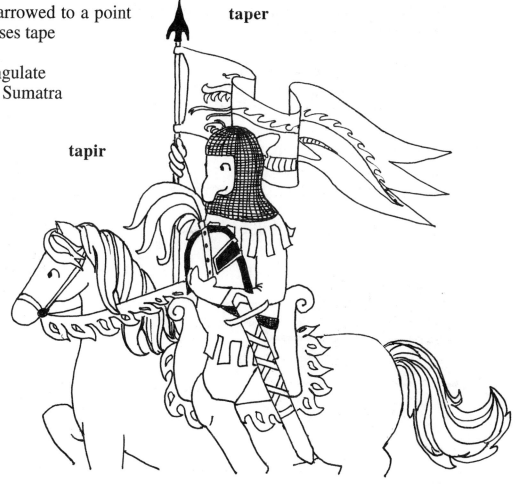

taper

tapir

702 **tarry**\TAIR ee\ v. to stay
terry\TAIR ee\ n. an absorbent cloth with loops

703 **tau**\TAH\ n. 19th letter of the Greek alphabet
taw\TAH\ v. to convert skin into leather by tanning

704 **taught**\TOT\ v. gave or received information,
taut\TOT\ adj. tightly pulled   v. to tangle
tot\TOT\ n. a young child

705 **teal**\TEEL\ adj. greenish blue
n. a small short-necked river duck
teel\TEEL\ n. sesame, also **til**

706 **team**\TEEM\ n. members
of a competitive group,
a crew, a matched pair of work animals
v. to work together
teem\TEEM\ v. to be full of, to swarm

taught

tot

tier

tear

707 **tear**\TEER\ n. a drop of salty liquid from an eye   v. to weep
tier\TEER\ n. a shelf, one layer above another

708 **teat**\TIT\ n. udder, nipple, also \TEET\
tit\TIT\ n. small long-tailed bird, an inferior horse, teat

709 **tenace**\TEN us\ n. in bridge, a combination
of two high cards, also \TEN ays\
tennis\TEN us\ n. a game played
with racquets and ball on a court

710 **tern**\TERN\ n. a type of seagull
terne\TERN\ n. a sheet of iron or steel coated with tin
turn\TERN\ n. a rotation, a bend v. to spin, to twist, to flip over

711 **terrene**\tuh REEN\ adj. earthly
tureen\tuh REEN\ n. a large soup bowl

712 **their**\THAIR\ pron. belongs to them
there\THAIR\ adv. in or at that place n. that position
they're\THAIR\ they are

713 **theirs**\THAIRZ\ pron. their part
there's\THAIRZ\ there is, there was

714 **threw**\THROO\ v. tossed, flung
through\THROO\ prep. in one side and out the other, finished, also **thru**

715 **throe**\THROHW\ n. a pang, a spasm
throw\THROHW\ n. the act of tossing, pitching v. to toss, to fling

thrown  throne

716 **throne**\THROHN\ n. the seat of a ruler   v. to hold kingly power
thrown\THROHN\ v. to have tossed, to have hurled

717 **thyme**\TIM\ n. a mint herb
time\TIM\ n. a measured period using a clock, the rate of speed
v. to schedule, to record the rate of speed

718 **tic**\TIK\ n. a twitching of a facial muscle
tick\TIK\ n. a wingless bloodsucking parasitic arachnid related to mites

719 **tical**\TIK ul\ n. an old Thai silver coin, current Thai money, also **tikal**
tickle\TIK ul\ n. a tingling prickling sensation
v. to excite nerves, to amuse, to please

720 **tide**\TID\ n. the rising and falling of the ocean twice a day, current   v. to flow or float on the tide, to get over an emergency
tied\TID\ v. fastened with a knot

tide

tied

721 **tighten**\TIT un\ v. to fasten more securely
titan\TIT un\ n. one of the legendary giants of Uranus and Gaea overthrown by the Olympian gods

722 **tighter**\TIT er\ adj. fit closer together, pulled more
titer\TIT er\ n. the strength of a solution, also **titre**

723 **til**\TIL\ n. sesame, also **teel**\TEEL\
till\TIL\ conj. until   n. a money box or drawer, a glacial drift prep. until   v. to cultivate soil, to plant and raise crops

724 **timber**\TIMB er\ n. lumber, trees or their wood
timbre\TIMB er\ n. the distinctive tone of a voice or instrument

725 **tincal**\TINK ul\ n. crude borax
tinkle\TINK ul\ n. a clinking sound   v. to make a high ringing noise

726 **titi**\TIT ee\ n. a South American monkey
tittie\TIT ee\ n. Scottish for sister

two   too

727 **to**\TOO\ adv. indicates direction   prep. used to show action, on, before
too\TOO\ adv. also, very
two\TOO\ adj. having two parts   n. the number 2

728 **toad**\TOHD\ n. an amphibian related to frogs, a detestable person
toed\TOHD\ adj. having so many toes, nail driven obliquely
towed\TOHD\ v. pulled along

729 **tocsin**\TOKS un\ n. an alarm bell
toxin\TOKS un\ n. a poisonous substance

730 tole\TOHL\ n. a decorative varnished board or tray
toll\TOHL\ n. a fee, a tax, the sound of a bell   v. to signal

731 ton\TUN\ n. a unit of weight equalling 2000 pounds
tun\TUN\ n. a barrel, a Mayan calendar year

732 tongue\TUNG\ n. the organ in the mouth
that tastes, takes in food, and forms
speech sounds, a pole of a wagon,
pin in a buckle, etc.
tung\TUNG\ n. a tree used to make varnish and oil

733 tool\TOOL\ n. an instrument, a machine
tulle\TOOL\ n. sheer silk, rayon, or nylon netting

734 toon\TOON\ adj. empty   n. a mahogany tree
of E. India and Australia
tune\TOON\ n. a melody, a tone
v. to adjust a receiver,
to adjust musical instruments

tongue

tung

735 tor\TOR\ n. a craggy hill
tore\TOR\ v. ripped
torr\TOR\ n. a raging flood

736 tort\TORT\ n. a civil crime except one involving breach of contract
torte\TORT\ n. a sugar and egg cake topped with fruit and nuts

737 tough\TUF\ adj. strong but flexible, stubborn   v. to endure
tuff\TUF\ n. rock made of fine volcanic ash

traiteur

traitor

738 traiteur\TRAYT er\ n. the keeper of a French or Italian restaurant
traitor\TRAYT er\ n. one who betrays another's trust

739 tray\TRAY\ n. a flat low rimmed plate
trey\TRAY\ n. a die with three spots, a card numbered three

740 troche\TROHK ee\ n. a medicinal tablet
trochee\TROHK ee\ n. an iambic meter /- or -/.

741 troop\TROOP\ n. a military group, a flock, a unit of scouts
v. to move in large numbers
troupe\TROOP\ n. a group of stage performers
v. to travel with a theatrical group

742 trooper\TROOP er\ n. one in the cavalry, a paratrooper, a policeman
trouper\TROOP er\ n. a member of a theatrical group

743 **turbit**\TER but\ n. a fancy short crested pigeon
turbot\TER but\ n. a large European flatfish

744 **typhous**\TI fus\ adj. relating to typhus
typhus\TI fus\ n. a serious disease transmitted by lice

745 **udder**\UD er\ n. a baglike milk-secreting organ
with two or more teats
utter\UD er\ adj. complete, absolute, also \UT er\

veil

746 **vail**\VAYL\ v. to lower
as a sign of respect
vale\VAYL\ n. a valley
veil\VAYL\ n. a cloth
covering the head and
shoulders, face netting,
a curtain   v. to cover with a veil

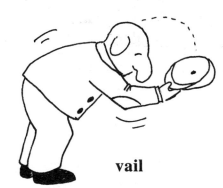

vail

747 **vain**\VAYN\ adj. conceited, futile
vane\VAYN\ n. a thin sheet of metal that turns to show wind
direction, turns a windmill, the flat part of a feather or arrow
vein\VAYN\ n. a blood vessel, a distinctive mood

748 **vary**\VAIR ee\ v. to change
very\VAIR ee\ adj. true, exact   adv. truly, to a high degree

749 vial\VI ul\ n.. a small container for liquid
vile\VI ul\ adj. wicked, terrible

750 vice\VIS\ n. a bad habit, defect, prostitution
vise\VIS\ n. a tool with jaws that grip
v. to hold with force

751 villain\VIL un\ n. a scoundrel,
the one who opposes the hero
villein\VIL un\ n. a free common villager,
also \vil AYN\

752 vinal\VIN ul\ adj. relating to wine
vinyl\VIN ul\ n. a plastic synthetic fabric
or floor covering

vile

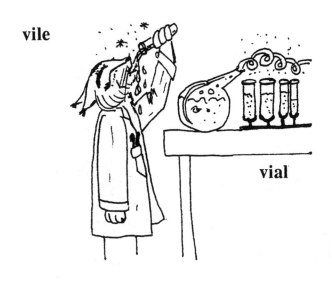

vial

753 wade\WAYD\ v. to walk in water,
to get to work with determination
weighed\WAYD\ v. considered,
found the heaviness of something

weighed

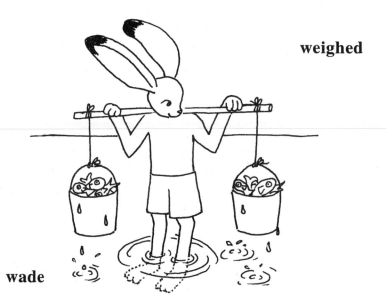

wade

754 **wail**\WAYL\ n. a cry v. to cry
wale\WAYL\ n. a welt, a ridge, a ship plank v. to choose
whale\WAYL\ n. a large mammal adapted to living in the ocean
v. to hit, to defeat soundly

755 **wain**\WAYN\ n. a heavy farm wagon
wane\WAYN\ n. the period from full moon to new moon,
a defect in lumber of the edge v. to dim, to lessen

waist

756 **waist**\WAYST\ n. the narrowest point
between neck and hips, the midpoint
of a ship
waste\WAYST\ adj. ruined,
worthless n. garbage, sewage, rejected
leftover material, a desert
v. to use carelessly or inefficiently

waste

TRASH

757 **wait**\WAYT\ n. a delay v. to stay in one place, to serve meals
weight\WAYT\ n. the heaviness of something

758 **waive**\WAYV\ v. to give up the right, to dismiss
wave\WAYV\ n. a moving ridge of water, an undulating movement
of energy, a hand moved back and forth v. to swing

759 waiver\WAYV er\ n. giving up the right to a claim, postponing a requirement
waver\WAYV er\ v. to weave, to have trouble deciding

760 waler\WAYL er\ n. an Australian saddle horse exported to India
whaler\WAYL er\ n. a person who hunts whales

wok

761 walk\WAHK\ n. going on foot for exercise, a sidewalk
v. to step, to move on foot
wok\WAHK\ n. a deep Chinese cooking pan for stir frying

walk

762 want\WAHNT\ n. the state
of lacking something
v. to need, to desire
wont\WAHNT\ adj. used to

763 war\WOR\ n. fighting between countries
or peoples   v. to fight
wore\WOR\ v. was dressed in,
carried, used up,

764 ware\WAIR\ n. goods
wear\WAIR\ n. clothing   v. to clothe,
to carry, to use
where\WAIR\ adv. at, in, in what place
n. what place, source, cause

765 water\WAHT er\ n. the liquid from clouds,
H2O   v. to give water
watter\WAHT er\ n. something having
a specified wattage

766 watt\WAHT\ n. a unit of power or a unit of work,
1/746 horsepower
what\WAHT\\WUT\ pron. used to ask

767 way\WAY\ n. a path, a method, a condition
weigh\WAY\ v. to measure on a scale,
to ponder, to count
whey\WAY\ n. the watery part of milk
separated from the curd in making cheese

768 we\WEE\ pron. plural of I
wee\WEE\ adj. tiny
whee\WEE\ interj. exclamation of delight

769 weak\WEEK\ adj. lacking strength, fragile
week\WEEK\ n. seven days

770 weal\WEEL\ n. a healthy state, a welt, also **wale**
we'll\WEEL\ we will, we shall
wheal\WHEEL\ n. site of itching, a welt
wheel\WHEEL\ n. a turning circular frame solid or spoked,
a disc   v. to turn on an axis, to roll

771 **wean**\WEEN\ v. to stop from nursing its mother's milk
wheen\WEEN\ n. a large amount

772 **weather**\WETH er\ n. temperature and rainfall conditions
wether\WETH er\ n. a castrated male sheep
whether\WETH er\ conj. either

weave  we've

We've been weaving for a whole hour!

773 **weave**\WEEV\ n. a pattern of interlaced threads
v. to make cloth on a loom
we've\WEEV\ we have

774 **we'd**\WEED\ we would, we should
weed\WEED\ n. a plant that grows without cultivation,
seaweed v. to get rid of unwanted things

775 **weet**\WEET\ v. to know
wheat\WEET\ n. a cereal grain ground into flour

776 **weir**\WEER\ n. a fence in a waterway to catch fish, a dam
we're\WEER\ we are, we were

777 **wen**\WEN\ n. a cyst, a rune that has become the modern English w
when\WEN\ adv. at what time   conj while
pron. what time   n. the time

778 **were**\WER\ v. past form of to be. We were here.
whir\WER\ n. a fluttering   v. to fly, to rotate rapidly, also **whirr**

wet

whet

Hey! Watch what you're doing, will you?

SPLASH! SPLASH!

779 **wet**\WET\ adj. damp, soaked, rainy   n. rain, water   v. to soak
whet\WET\ v. to sharpen

780 whaup\WOP\ n. a European curlew
whop\WOP\ v. to defeat, to hit

781 which\WICH\ pron. what one, used to ask for a decision
witch\WICH\ n. an ugly hag, a sorceress

782 whig\WIL\ n. member or supporter of a British political party
wig\WIL\ n. a hairpiece

783 while\WIL\ conj. during   n. a period of time   v. to pass time
wile\WIL\ n. a trick   v. to lure, to pass time

784 whin\WIN\ n. a hard rock, basalt,
a spiny yellow-flowered shrub
win\WIN\ v. to be first, to succeed

wine

whine

The service here stinks! Whose idea was it to come here anyway? I hate this place...

785 whine\WIN\ n. a high pitched cry
v. to complain
wine\WIN\ n. fermented grape juice,
fermented fruit juice   v. to serve wine
wyne\WIN\ v. to haw, to turn left

786 whining\WIN\ ing\ v. complaining, crying
wining\WIN ing\ v. treating one's friends to wine

787 **whish**\WISH\ n. a rushing sound   v. to make a rushing sound, to move at high speed
wish\WISH\ n. a request, a goal   v. to want, to crave

788 **whist**\WIST\ adj. quiet   n. a card game related to bridge
wist\WIST\ 16 or 18 acres in Sussex, 60 acres in Anglo Saxon times

white

wight

789 **white**\WIT\ adj. colorless   n. the color of greatest lightness   v. to cut
wight\WIT\ adj. strong, swift   n. a living creature
wite\WIT\ n. a fine paid to an English king for serious crimes,
an exemption from paying the fine   v. to punish, also **wyte**

790 **whittle**\WIT ul\ n. a large knife v. to carve slowly with a knife
wittol\WIT ul\ n. a man who allows his wife to cheat on him

791 **whoa**\WOH\ interj. command to stop, also \HOH\
woe\WOH\ n. sorrow, state of grief interj. expresses sorrow, distress

792 **who's**\HOOZ\ who is, who was, who has
whose\HOOZ\ pron. asking to whom does this belong?

793 **wind**\WIND\ n. a winch v. to coil, to wrap around and around
wynd\WIND\ n. a narrow alley v. to turn left, also **wyne**

794 wins\WINZ\ v. overcomes, defeats
winze\WINZ\ n. a vertical or steep passageway in a mine   v. to curse

795 wit\WIT\ n. intelligence, a talent for amusing
whit\WIT\ n. the smallest part

796 with\WITH\ prep. shows accompaniment, combination, or manner
withe\WITH\ n. a thin branch used as a rope

797 wood\WUD\ n. a group of trees, lumber
would\WUD\ v. prefers

worst

wurst

798 worst\WERST\ adj. the most unfavorable, the most painful
wurst\WERST\ n. sausage

799 **yawn**\YON\ n. an involuntary deep breath, a gap
yon\YON\ adj. over there   pron that or those

800 **yogh**\YOHK\ n. a letter in Middle English, also \YOHG\
yoke\YOHK\ n. a wooden bar attached to animals' necks for pulling,
a pair of oxen   v. to hitch up a team of oxen
yolk\YOHK\ n. the yellow part of an egg

yule

you'll

801 **you'll**\YOOL\ you will
yule\YOOL\ n. Christmas

802 **yore**\YOR\ n. a long time ago
your\YOR\ pron. belongs to you
you're\YOR\ you are, you were

803 **zinc**\ZINK\ n. a bluish-white crystalline metallic element
v. to treat or coat with zinc, to galvanize
zink\ZINK\ n. a cornet, also **zinke** \ZINK uh\

Index

very 748
vial 749
vice 750
vile 749
villain 751
villein 751
vinal 752
vinyl 752
vise 750
wade 753
wail 754
wain 755
waist 756
wait 757
waive 758
waiver 759
wale 754
waler 760
walk 761
wane 755
want 762
war 763
ware 764
waste 756
water 765
watt 766
watter 765
wave 758
waver 759
way 767
we 768
we'd 774
we'll 770
we're 776
we've 773
weak 769
weal 770
wean 771
wear 764
weather 772
weave 773
wee 768
weed 774
week 769
weet 775
weigh 767

weighed 753
weight 757
weir 776
wen 777
were 778
wet 779
wether 772
whale 754
whaler 760
what 766
whaup 780
wheal 770
wheat 775
whee 768
wheel 770
wheen 771
when 777
where 764
whet 779
whether 772
whey 767
which 781
whig 782
while 783
whin 784
whine 785
whining 786
whir 778
whish 787
whist 788
whit 795
white 789
whittle 790
who's 791
whoa 357
whoa 792
whole 362
wholly 363
whop 780
whore 358
whose 791
wig 782
wight 789
wile 783
win 784
wind 793

wine 785
wining 786
wins 794
winze 794
wish 787
wist 788
wit 795
witch 781
wite 789
with 796
withe 796
wittol 790
woe 792
wok 761
won 489
wont 762
wood 797
wore 763
worst 798
would 797
wrack 556
wracks 558
wraith 569
wrap 566
wrapped 567
wrath 570
wreak 580
wreck 579
wrecks 586
wrest 582
wretch 583
wright 591
wring 592
wringer 593
write 591
wrote 606
wrought 605
wrung 610
wry 611
wurst 798
wynd 793
wyne 785
xat 135
yawn 799
yew 257
yogh 800

yoke 800
yolk 800
yon 799
yore 801
you 257
you'll 802
you're 801
your 801
yule 802
zinc 803
zink 803

Send your homophone pair to:
Lynx Links
P.O. Box 754
Brush Prairie, WA 98606